The Talent Genius -

How the Top 1% of Realtors
Build World-Class Teams

by:

John Pyke

Copyright

LinkedIn: https://www.linkedin.com/in/thetalentgenius
Website: www.thetalentgenius.com
Email: johnapyke@gmail.com

1st Edition 2016
First Published 2016 for John Pyke
by Evolve Global Publishing
PO Box 327 Stanhope Gardens NSW 2768
info@evolveglobalpublishing.com
www.evolveglobalpublishing.com

Book Layout: © 2016 Evolve Global Publishing

ISBN: (Paperback) 9781684186518
ISBN-13: (Createspace) 978-1539779230
ISBN-10: (Createspace) 1539779238
ISBN: (Smashwords) 9781370625253
ASIN: (Amazon Kindle) B01M3SLG6N

This book is available on Barnes & Noble, Kobo, Apple iBooks (digital), Google Books (digital)

Table of Contents

The Talent Genius - How the Top 1% of Realtors Build World-
Class Teams:
More Advance Praise 7

Section I - Why Hire Slow, Fire Fast is a Bad Strategy............. 13
Chapter 1- The Monster Problem 15
Chapter 2 - Scientific Weapons Hiding in Plain Sight............... 24

Section II - How to Hire Consistent Top Performers................ 33
Chapter 3 - Find the Right Talent Pool 35
Chapter 4 - Values and Motivators 40
Chapter 5 - Select Those Hardwired for Success 45
Chapter 6 - Interview Only Top Performers—Check for
Chemistry, Culture, and Commitment 50

Section III - After You Hire Fast, What Comes Next?................ 61
Chapter 7 - Accelerate Onboarding.. 63
Chapter 8 - The Hire Fast Fire Fast Checklist 75
Final Thoughts... 78

Section IV - Bonus Chapters – Important Considerations........ 81
Chapter 9 - Differentiation – A Compelling,
Unique Selling Proposition 83
Chapter 10 - Get LinkedIn or Get Left Out............................... 87
Chapter 11 - Coaching – Accelerate Your
Learning and Success.. 92
Chapter 12 - Wealth Mastery - Protect and
Leverage Your Money... 96

Section V - Recommendations – Best Real Estate Resources.. 107
Corcoran Coaching and Consulting... 109
Entertainment® – VIP Perks 110
LinkedIn.. 111
Pacific Advisors, Inc.. 112
Radio and Television Experts (RATE) 114
Vyral Marketing 115
Appendix A - Literature Review................................. 116
Appendix B - Acknowledgments 121
Appendix C - About the Author................................. 124

The Talent Genius - How the Top 1% of Realtors Build World-Class Teams: More Advance Praise

"John Pyke aka "The Talent Genius" helped me grow from solo agent to seventh level in three years - I will be retiring in five months on my birthday. This year we are on track to sell over 425 sides (close to double last year's production) and we will earn the distinction of being among The Top 250 Real Estate firms in the country as rated by The Wall Street Journal Real Trends. John's "Done For Your Hiring System" is the best investment I have made in my real estate business. He has helped me create true leverage by building a team that is now over 30 people strong and growing and he has significantly improved the quality of my life – I highly recommend John!"

- Tom Daves, Tom Daves Team & #1 Keller Willams Agent for four consecutive years

"John Pyke is my secret weapon! John's services are invaluable in assessing agents and deciding where my time and efforts will be best spent. Consistently hiring the best people is unquestionably the single most important ingredient for success – the smaller the team the more important is it to have the best talent. John takes care of all my human capital needs. I am so appreciative of his expertise and would not want to face a single year without him!"

- Marti Hampton, RE/MAX One Realty & Top 10 Worldwide for RE/MAX since 2007

"John eliminates the costly, frustrating guesswork associated with hiring and helps us consistently hire top performers. With his help, we have grown from one office to four offices. In 2014 and 2015 we sold 378 and 555 sides respectively. Last year we were ranked by The Wall Street Journal Real Trends in the Top 30 Real Estate firms in the United States. This year we are on track to sell over 750 homes. John's time-tested, scientifically proven hiring system delivers unmatched results - I highly recommend him!"

- Jeff Cook, Jeff Cook Real Estate - Wall Street Journal Top 30 Real Estate Team in U.S. 2015

"Thank you John Pyke! You have been an amazing addition to our team! Your incredible time-tested, scientifically proven hiring process has saved us tons of time, money and frustration. We no longer interview the wrong people or make costly hiring mistakes. You accurately predict who will be a mediocre performer and who will be a superstar! You have attracted hundreds of applicants and narrowed down the list to the best fit for our team. We wish we would have found you years ago. For anyone struggling with consistently hiring the best talent, like we used to, I highly recommend John – he delivers outstanding results."

- Lisa Burridge, Associate Broker, ABR, CRS, Wall Street Journal/Real Trends Ranked #18 Nationally

"John Pyke and his ability to find us the most qualified candidates has been nothing short of amazing for our business. With John's knowledge and insight we have grown from a team of 5 to a team of 11 in just 12 months. One of our new hires sold $18.46M in his first year with us – I highly recommend John!"

- Chad Schwendeman, EXIT Lakes Realty Premier, #1 Agent out of 25,000+ in North America and Ranked #27 Nationally by Wall Street Journal Real Trends for 2015

"We have worked with John Pyke for many years. His advice has been instrumental in our growth from a few people to a large team of 26 that is ranked #147 on the Real Trends, Wall Street Journal list of top producing Teams in the United States. Hiring the right people is critical to our growth and continued success. John gives us the insight we need to make wise hiring decisions. Prior to using his services we made many costly mistakes in our hiring practices. We even consult with John when we are contemplating promotions or altering a team mate's responsibilities. He can help us promote strategically and make sure we are using everyone's talents to the fullest. He is like a trusted member of our team. His value far exceeds the investment.

- Tami Holmes, Tami Holmes Real Estate Experts - HER Realty, Ranked #147 Nationally

"Owning and running a business in Alaska can be challenging, especially with finding, hiring and retaining top talent. We struggled for years to do this on our own in what seemed like a shallow talent pool with a transient work force. Something needed to change. We knew we needed a consistent, repeatable system for finding amazing talent for our team if we were to succeed, but didn't have the expertise to do so. Then we hired John Pyke. John has helped us set up this system for our company and it has been a game changer. His insight and mentorship has provided us guidance and leverage in an area where having an expert giving you advice is priceless. If human capital is your company's #1 asset like we believe ours to be, hire John and his team immediately and get your on-boarding process ready!"

- Wes Madden, Madden Real Estate - Wall Street Journal Top 50 Real Estate Team in U.S. 2010-2015

"John Pyke has an amazing system for finding great talent for our organization! With his help, we are much better able to make sure that we place the right people in the right positions to help our business grow so that we, in turn, can better serve our community – I wholeheartedly recommend John!"

- Holli McCray, The Holli McCray Group - 2015 Wall Street Journal/Real Trends Ranked #92 Nationally

"I met John Pyke from one of my real estate clients Jason Bramblett, who said "Matt there is a guy you need to bring to our network - he is a talent head hunter that is unlike anyone I've ever met that would bring real value to our group." Well, that was an understatement. As the president of a marketing ad agency that works with the largest collective group of top real estate agents advertising on radio and television, I'm always looking for ways to add value. Recruiting campaigns on radio has always been successful for us - but with John he adds a whole new dimension. Since we may generate 45-60 candidates, John assesses them with scientifically proven tools and targets the top 3-4 superstars, thus saving the agent hours, days, and weeks away from their business interviewing weak prospects. John has been a pleasure to work with and genuinely cares about the success of every single client we send to him. His advice has consistently been spot on and has helped many of our agents grow because of this. We highly value our relationship."

- Matt Wagner, President, Radio And Television Experts LLC

"For all intents and purposes, John is the HR department for our team. He creates job advertisements and is the first point of defense weeding through applications and making sure we only interview the best of the best. He helps us understand what things we are looking for in each position/candidate, as well as helps us understand our own personality traits and how to interact with each other. His expertise is a priceless asset to our company. Hire John today!"

- Tara Limbird, Limbird Real Estate Group - 2015 Wall Street Journal Real Trends Ranked #51 Nationally

Section I

Why Hire Slow, Fire Fast is a Bad Strategy

Chapter 1
The Monster Problem

Does this sound familiar? You are a leader with an opening on your sales team. Every moment you do not fill that opening, you are literally losing money; you need someone right now. But you don't want to rush it. You post the position on all the right job boards, or perhaps you even reach out to a recruiter. The stack of resumes hits your desk and you pore over them, spending hours of what should be productive time, trying to read between the lines to find that special something that spells success. Maybe you give candidates a personality test to get an extra dimension of information about them, but you don't feel much closer to the right answer.

But even when you take all that time—selecting candidates, interviewing, calling references, and training—you still have no assurance that the person you hired will have what it takes to be a consistent top performer. Let's face it: hiring a new employee is risky. It's a crapshoot, a coin flip, a dart toss. Even when you do everything right, there is no guarantee that your new hire will be the right fit. When it does work out, it feels more like random chance than anything you can control. The process of hiring staff can be time-consuming, frustrating, and costly, but there is a better way to quadruple your hiring success from 20 percent or less to 80 percent or more using a time-tested, proven science.

There is an old Chinese proverb that says, "If you want to be successful, ask those coming back." The purpose of this book is to share how to hire and build a world-class sales team using a time-tested, scientifically proven set of processes.

These processes or best practices are the driving force behind many of the top 250 residential real estate teams in the country – the elite 1% as ranked by the Wall Street Journal Real Trends. My hope is that the insights in this book will help you dramatically accelerate your own success. Since the principles and truths in this book are universal, every company, regardless of industry, has the potential to benefit significantly from the unmatched outcomes these processes deliver. Eleanor Roosevelt said it best, "Learn from the mistakes of others. You can't live long enough to make them all yourself." Learning from the experiences of others is one of the best ways to quickly elevate your results. From both personal experience and my experience of working with countless clients, investing in Mastermind Groups and securing expert help from coaches or consultants is some of the absolute best time and money well spent.

A significant part of this book will address the single greatest challenge and opportunity for all business owners and entrepreneurs – consistently hiring top performing people. Why? The Gallup organization found that "Recruiting is the HR function with the highest impact on revenue. Excellent recruiting practices contribute to more than three times revenue growth and two times profit margin."

Hire Slow, Fire Fast

You have probably heard the oft-repeated, now-cliché phrase: "Hire Slow, Fire Fast." On the surface it seems like a good strategy. Taking a thorough, unrushed approach to hiring allows a company to really understand if the person they hire has the skills and cultural fit to succeed at their organization. They will have time to determine that a person is stable, committed, and fits in with the team, not to mention the opportunity to craft the perfect offer to entice them to join the company.

Likewise, if it turns out that a mistake was made and someone is not working out, they can quickly and humanely fire them.

But the reality is often quite different. A slow hiring process takes valuable time away from the main focus of business and sucks up other valuable resources as well. If that job sits empty for too long, you risk major losses in overall productivity, especially if other team members are burdened with picking up the slack. Often, you don't have the luxury of that kind of time, especially if you are a start-up or looking to scale your business quickly.

Many leaders do not feel confident that they have found that elusive perfect hire. This is why they stall and call it "being selective." Not to mention, leading candidates along while you essentially drag your feet is going to encourage top performers to look elsewhere. That sort of wishy-washy behavior is deeply unattractive to the very people you wish to bring in.

Incidentally, the "fire fast" bit of the adage does ring true. You don't want to waste too much time on someone who isn't going to succeed. Sometimes employers feel that an employee just needs the right training or development to help them make it, but the truth is, traditional training rarely makes any difference. Unless the employee has the fundamental, innate attributes to be a success in their role, there is very little to be done to fix that.

Our brains are extraordinary. The typical brain consists of some 100 billion cells, each of which connects and communicates with up to 10,000 of its colleagues. Together they forge an elaborate network of some one quadrillion (1,000,000,000,000,000) connections that guides how we talk, eat, breathe, and move[1]. James Watson, who won the Nobel Prize for helping discover DNA, escribed the human brain as "the most complex thing we have yet discovered in our universe."

---

[1] Pink, Daniel H. A Whole New Mind: Why Right-brainers Will Rule the Future. New York: Riverhead Books, 2006.

Why Don't Traditional Hiring Strategies Work?

Have you ever wondered why your highest-performing employees are your highest-performing employees? If you could identify that special something, perhaps you could recognize it in your prospective employees as well. How can you know with certainty if a candidate has what it takes to be a consistent top performer? Is there a way to find out quickly before wasting time and resources on someone that will never measure up?

The human brain is incredibly complex—what you are able to observe outwardly about a person you are evaluating is barely scratching the surface. It is like an iceberg, where 88 percent of it is hidden below the surface. In a typical interview scenario, you are only able to see a small amount of someone's true nature and potential. Interviewing is both art and science, and most people are not professional interviewers; in fact, the majority of candidates are quite poor at interviewing. Most hiring managers are also not that skilled at asking the right questions, so the likelihood of getting the most useful and revealing information from an interview is quite low.

If someone is a poor interviewer, that doesn't necessarily mean they are not the best person for the job. Conversely, the smoothest, most charming candidate may not be the right person either, because the things you need to know go much deeper than the average interview can reach. You need to know the things that are fundamental to their nature: persistence, drive, initiative, handling rejection, self-discipline, work ethic, ability to problem-solve, and perhaps, most importantly of all, the ability to connect on an emotional level to quickly and easily build trust and rapport. Since these are innate talents that cannot be learned or taught, you need a way to discover the hidden potential of every candidate. Using a time-tested, scientifically proven way to access the 88 percent of what is hidden is the surest way to eliminate the costly, frustrating guesswork associated with hiring and equips you to consistently make the best hiring decisions.

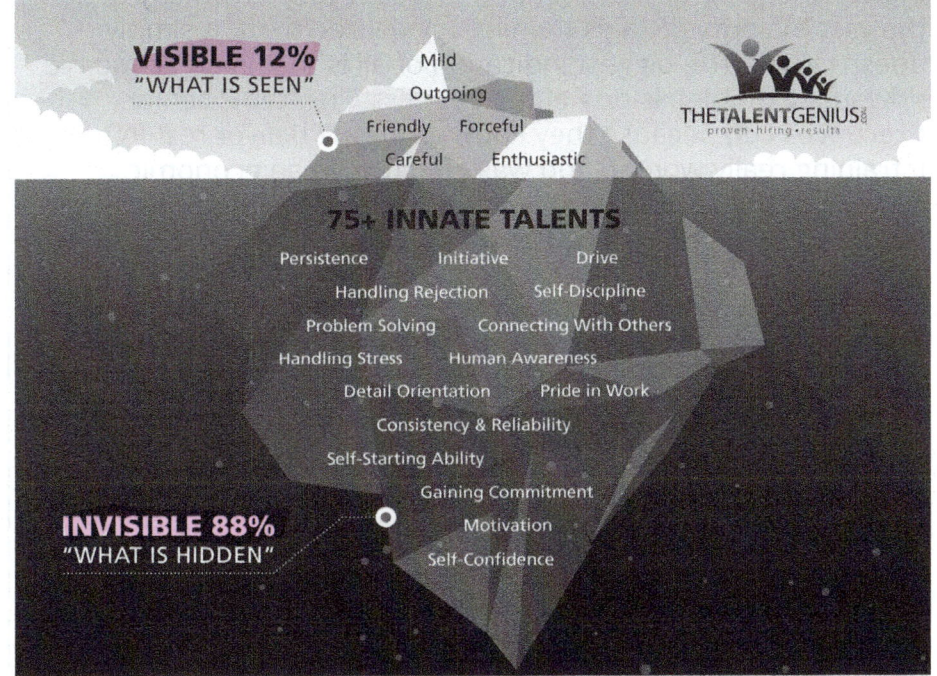

Traditional Training Doesn't Work

After having helped train over 200,000 people and participating in over 100 programs personally, I can authoritatively say the vast majority of sales training is legalized theft. It simply doesn't work. The biggest indication of all is that in an economic downturn, training is one of the very first line items senior executives cut, because they know it doesn't deliver results. If training really worked and was effective, in an economic downturn, they would double and triple down and do more training and development. It's the opposite.

The truth is, only rarely is there a direct link between training and an increase in sales. Training can be helpful for people who are already predisposed to be good at the job. If you train someone who already has the innate talent to succeed, my experience is they will deliver sales growth six times the growth of the average performers. If you train someone who is mediocre, you will have a barely noticeable lift in productivity, and likely they will forget just about all of what they learned in thirty days.

Most training is just training. It does not start with an assessment to gauge where the participants are operating from or give them any insight into what they are good at. Most of the time, training is focused on a person's weakness, which is a negative reinforcement of what they are not good at and not how to improve. It is a waste of time, a waste of resources, and gives many participants a bad impression of themselves.

In most cases, if someone is a poor performer, it isn't that they lack education or training. It is that they lack the innate abilities that would allow them to succeed in that role. For instance, if they are a salesperson but it makes them very uncomfortable to reach out to new prospects and they don't have the force of will to close the sale, no amount of training will fix that.

Take the Guesswork Out of It

When you implement a time-tested, proven hiring system that utilizes scientifically validated data, you can take the subjectivity and guesswork out of hiring.

This book will show you how to use assessments to identify the right candidates quickly and allow you to feel supremely confident about your decision. After all, knowing is always better than guessing.

How do I know this? I have been passionate about this topic since college and I've invested my twenty-five-year career studying why some people succeed and others fail.

What I've found is that there are certain innate abilities that people have, and when they are in a position that aligns with their true nature, they are wildly successful. The great part is, you can identify those qualities before you hire someone—and it can be done quickly and easily.

The "Done-For-You Hiring System" relies on a three-part assessment to identify a person's personality, motivators, and talents. This allows you to weed out those who are not hardwired for success before you waste any time with them. After that, you merely need to identify the cultural fit of a candidate in order to know they will be a success.

Many executives I have met with over the years felt like this was just another scheme that wouldn't yield anything of value. For instance, I was working with a company by the name of Utility Service. ⚹ PAUL

The company had an extremely long, demanding training program—it was about two years of salary and benefits before they found out whether the new hire could sell or not.

Undeterred, I went to one of his regional vice presidents and asked him to select three sales people—his best, his worst, and someone in between—and using my system, I could identify which one was which based on the assessments alone. I was right, and the vice president was floored.

Since they were so heavily invested in them by that point, they usually kept them around. I approached the senior vice president and told him I had the solution to his problems. That seasoned Fortune 500 SVP essentially showed me the door.

He went to the senior vice president who had turned me down and told him this was the most unbelievable thing he had ever seen. He said, "John not only told me why my high performer is my high performer. He told me why the other one is performing poorly right now. He knows more about my people than I know after having worked with them for four years. We have to do this!"

The senior vice president was still a little skeptical, but they retained me to evaluate their current staff. I assessed all forty salespeople and selected the ten whom I thought were the top performers. Nine of the ten salespeople I chose had sold 80 percent of the total sales revenue over the last four years. The clients were impressed, but I did wonder why I hadn't entirely nailed it. It turned out, the tenth person I identified—who had the best profiles of any of them—was a new hire.

By his second year, he was the top salesperson in the entire company and sold over seven million dollars' worth of business, which is more than seven times what most salespeople sell in their second year. Turns out I was ten for ten after all. That senior vice president thought I walked on water after that and decided to use the same proven science to eliminate his costly 80 percent sales turnover rate.

I am used to people being skeptical of this approach. But I am so confident in it that many times, I will even make a wager and offer to pay five thousand dollars if I can't identify the highest performer from the lowest performer. Why do I make this wager? Because I have never been wrong.

The validity and reliability of the tools allows me to predict, with laser-like accuracy, who has the sales DNA and who doesn't. The contrast between the results of the highest and the lowest are so dramatic it is impossible to be wrong.

You, too, can tap into this incredible source of information and hire with complete confidence. In the chapters ahead, I will describe:

- What the scientific assessments evaluate
- How to interview top performers for cultural fit
- How to leverage an employee's innate strengths
- How to accelerate the onboarding process

In the next chapter, we will look at these time-tested, scientifically proven breakthroughs you can deploy. Having the capability to identify the hidden talents and motivators of top performers has the potential to quadruple your hiring success, secure significant competitive advantage, and grow top-line sales revenues to record levels.

Chapter 2

Scientific Weapons Hiding in Plain Sight

What is the solution to this monster problem? Science!

All the typical wisdom about hiring is wrong. Experience, age, education—or lack thereof—have absolutely nothing to do with predicting a job candidate's performance. Using time-tested, scientifically validated instruments will conservatively give you 80 percent of the information you need to make the best hiring decision. The method is based on statistical data that has consistently proven to be four times more effective than typical hiring methods. The other 20 percent comes down to chemistry: Is this person a good cultural fit with your organization? Will he or she be a good team member? Does the person match the values of the company?

The first step is using assessments to find the top 10 percent of talent that are hardwired for high performance for a specific position. Only then will you check for cultural fit.

My Story

As I said in the first chapter, discovering the reason why some people consistently perform at the highest levels, and most don't, has been a passion my entire career. These ideas stem from over twenty-five years of research into performance in the workplace.

My MBA thesis was called, "Intrinsic Versus Extrinsic Motivational Factors Impacting a Person's Performance," but what it really is about is why some people succeed and most people fail. I was looking to understand if performance was internally driven—someone is born to succeed—or externally driven—success is molded by how the person is managed and the culture of the company. From my observations, I learned that it is not one or the other, but a combination of the two. I have found that both internal and external factors matter immensely in determining an employee's success.

Here is an example of what I mean. I recently helped a company hire a senior executive. Jim's first six months on the job were absolutely brilliant. The company was thrilled and thought I was a genius for finding this perfect fit. The second six months were a total contrast—his performance just tanked. The other executives didn't know what to make of it. Was this even the same guy? They brought me back in to try to figure out what had happened. I knew from my work to hire him that Jim valued autonomy and freedom above all else. He was motivated by being trusted to make good decisions and by having a boss that gave him support when he needed it.

When I talked to Jim, I found out that on month seven, he got a new boss. This boss was one of the most awful micromanagers the world has ever seen. Jim valued his autonomy, and this guy was always checking up on him— telling him what to do, when to do it, and how to do it. It was so bad, Jim told me, "During my breaks, I go to the parking lot, sit in my car, look at the gas gauge and wonder how far that amount of gas would take me from this company. It is that awful a work environment for me now."

Here you have an employee who is exceptional. But then he gets a leader who is an absolute tyrant and he can't function in that kind of environment, so his performance drops like a rock.

When I explained this, the company leadership had him report to a different leader and Jim started to soar again.

After my graduate work, my second job was working in the consumer packaged goods industry with a company called Alberto Culver. When I started, the company had a big problem with their customer base: there had been four sales reps in the last two years in the territory, and the lack of continuity and response had taken a toll. A significant number of past customers wouldn't even let me meet with them because they figured, "What's the point? You'll be gone in six months, too." This was a challenge, but I was driven to succeed. I worked with customers to fix their problems, replace damaged products, and listened to their needs. I quickly won their respect and trust, which translated into sales, and I became the number one salesperson at the company in my first year.

From there, I went on to McNeil Consumer Products, a division of Johnson & Johnson—one of the top three consumer packaged goods companies in the industry. This was the big leagues. I was replacing someone who had been promoted, and the territory had been vacant for four months. Again, not a great situation, but within eight months I had the highest sales increase of anybody on the sales team.

After two years with McNeil, I became the national sales manager of a company that provided outsourced sales teams for companies that had remote territories where it didn't make sense to have a full-time salesperson. I was responsible for the Kodak account, which was worth 20 million dollars in camera and film sales.

From there, I went to Learning International, one of the world's leading sales training organizations. While I was the youngest person they had ever hired, in my first year, my sales output was more than anyone in the history of the company.

Some of what I know about training and development I learned working there; however, I started to have an ethical dilemma—the realization that there was no direct causal link between the training and an increase in sales. Although hugely successful in selling these training programs, my feelings were that I wasn't being totally honest.

This set me on a quest to really understand why some people consistently perform on a high level and others do not. In 1995, I moved to Greensboro, North Carolina, and learned from the life's work of one of the co-founders of The Center for Creative Leadership (CCL). CCL is one of the top leadership companies in the world, and their teachings are based on the foundation of self-awareness. CCL works primarily with high-performing executives, high potential mid-managers, or executives who have derailed in order to salvage their careers. CCL uses psychometric tools and extensive feedback from their peers, leaders, and subordinates to better understand the impact of their actions and make them more aware of the consequences of those actions.

I started to work with several leadership consultants who had been mentored by the founders of the Center for Creative Leadership. While working there, I met an entrepreneur who was selling a compelling solution to better develop existing salespeople. His system was far superior because it was based on assessments. His program was centered on the idea that people are not all the same, so you have to find out what makes them tick before you train them. I was so impressed by this that I joined his team, became director of sales in my second month, and sold nearly half of the total sales revenue of the company out of eight people in my first ten months. While at this organization I helped the owner reinvent his company.

Thinking about all my own research and the assessment-based training, I had an epiphany.

It was clear to me that each individual's success is a unique blend of personality style and innate talents motivated by the values they hold dear. Using time-tested, scientifically proven assessments, we could hone in on the people who are hardwired for success.

The System

The assessment is actually three separate instruments—separate, but inseparable. Each piece measures different things, but all three are needed for a complete, advanced insight into a candidate's ability to perform. Here are the three areas:

1. Personality style
2. Values and motivation
3. Innate talents or strengths

The assessments we use are completed online, and the results generate about seventy pages of data—we know the candidate more than they know themselves by the end of it. This information can then be compared with people working in that type of job who are performing at the highest levels.

Personality style: While there are many personality assessments available today, DiSC is the best one for these purposes. The original tenets were codified by psychologist William Marston in the 1920s and then were turned into an assessment instrument in the 1950s. There are four dimensions: Dominance (D), Influence (I), Steadiness (S), and Conscientiousness (C). Most people are a combination of all of these dimensions, but tend to most favor one or two quadrants. This is a solid instrument, though not all DiSC profiles are created equal, so you must choose between them carefully.

Values and motivation: This assessment identifies what values motivate a person's behaviors, which is helpful in identifying the type of job a person will succeed in. Each person has values associated with core dimensions, but each person's distribution amongst the values is unique. Certain motivators will be excellent predictors of consistent high performance. As you evaluate potential candidates, you will want to be sure that their top and bottom motivating factors align with the position and environment of your organization. The "why" of human performance is a major part of the equation; when properly understood and implemented, this can assist with workplace engagement and overall satisfaction.

Innate talents and strengths: This assessment is based on the work of Dr. Robert Hartman, a German logician and philosopher whose primary area of study was axiology, the study of value. Essentially, he felt all good things share a common formal or structural pattern, but that all good things are not equal. Therefore "how" we value is just as important as "what" we value. Jay Niblick, a leading expert who specializes in unlocking a person's genius and finding ways to maximize it, was inspired to build on Hartman's theories. After undertaking extensive study of successful people in many fields, he identified that people have certain strengths which are ingrained and unchangeable. By working with those strengths instead of against them, people can become top performers. The assessment identifies the innate talents that ought to be present for different positions.

People Usually Only Change in the Movies

Another crucial insight I have learned from years of research in this area is that the vast majority of the people do not change, even when their job—or even their life—depends on it. Consider the following research study of individuals who underwent a quadruple bypass surgery.

In an article in Fast Company entitled, "Change or Die,[1]" Alan Deutschman revealed some research with literal life and death implications - the inability of a patient to change lifestyle to save his or her life. The author says, "What if a well-informed, trusted authority figure said you had to make difficult and enduring changes in the way you think and act? If you didn't, your time would soon end - a lot sooner than it had to. Could you change when...it mattered most? Here are the... scientifically studied odds: nine to one.

That's nine to one against you." If ninety percent of patients who have already undergone bypass surgery due to severe heart disease are unable to change their behaviors with life-and-death consequences hanging in the balance, how and why would we possibly expect underperforming people to change? In a Harvard Business Review article titled "How Hardwired is Human Behavior," Nigel Nicholson put it this way: "Accept that people cannot demonstrate leadership qualities they don't innately possess, even if the business situation urgently demands it."[2]

Translating this to business, how many times have you had employees who are doing poorly, who you have placed into a "performance improvement plan" to try and change or improve their results? Have you ever found someone who is able to flick a switch and suddenly become a consistent high performer in that specific area? Of course not—the vast majority of time, they get fired. Or they hang on for years barely achieving any meaningful results.

From my experience, people usually only change in the movies. Other than a supernatural act of God or a traumatic, life-altering event like the death of a loved one or a divorce, people pretty much stay the same. In fact, over time, people usually become more like they already are. For example, if someone has the tendency to be impatient, over time, their lack of patience becomes more pronounced or frequent.

The point is that comfort zones are incredibly powerful and over time people typically become even more settled in their behaviors and ways of doing things. As a result, the focus should not be on changing someone but making sure their personality, motivators and innate talents are closely aligned with what the job requires to be successful.

The inability of most people to change is another critical reason underscoring the importance and urgency of hiring the best person the first time, every time! Always be on the lookout for talented people - the ones who are compelling who make a positive impression. This book will help you virtually eliminate all the frustrating, costly guesswork associated with hiring and replace it with certainty.

---

[1] https://www.fastcompany.com/52717/change-or-die
[2] Nigel Nicholson. "How Hardwired Is Human Behavior?" Harvard Business Review 76, no. 4 (July/August 1998): 134-47.

Section II
How to Hire Consistent Top Performers

Chapter 3
Find the Right Talent Pool

How can you improve your hiring decisions from the realm of chance to a place of confidence? Rather than rolling the dice and hoping for the best, you must assess candidates using thoroughly researched and tested scientific principles. Many organizations use some form of testing as part of their hiring practices, but according to a 2014 Aberdeen Group research study, only 14 percent of organizations have any data to measure the effectiveness of their assessment strategy. They continue to leave it mostly to chance.

Most people have taken a personality test at some point in their careers, be it on paper or online. These are often given as part of team-building seminars to help people understand one another's differences and work together more effectively. Such tests can be revealing, but used on their own in the hiring process, they are not more effective than traditional hiring methods. Professor Frank Schmidt, professor emeritus at the University of Iowa, analyzed workplace hiring data from the last hundred years and revealed that personality tests alone were only slightly more helpful as a predictor of future job performance than looking at just a resume alone. On the other hand, his landmark study found that "multi-measure tests"— those that incorporated cognitive ability, personality, and integrity—showed the highest correlation between test scores and predicted job performance (For more information, see the literature review in Appendix A).

This concept is what I discovered years ago through my own work, and this proven assessment system incorporates three areas to create a comprehensive picture of the candidate. All of these areas must be evaluated together to determine how a potential employee will perform.

1. Personality assessment
2. Values and motivation
3. Innate talents and strengths

In this chapter, we will look at the first area to see why you should know about this aspect of potential employees.

Personality Assessment with DiSC

There are many personality tests out there, most based on the four-quadrant principle, which posits that people can be divided into four different personality types, and most individuals are some combination of the four. This type of assessment goes back as far as Ancient Greece, when the philosopher Empedocles coined the idea of the four classical elements—Earth, Water, Air, and Fire—that make up everything in the cosmos. This concept has been pretty popular ever since, with varying takes on it over the millennia.

It can be overwhelming then to choose among these assessments, but I have found that the DiSC profile system is the best for an accurate gauge in this process. The DiSC system isn't ancient, but it has been in use for many decades.

William Moulton Marston—the father of DiSC—was a Harvard-educated physiological psychologist who had early success as the inventor of the polygraph machine (more commonly known as a lie-detector test). He was particularly interested in how emotions lead to behavioral differences in groups of people, and his 1928 book, Emotions of Normal People, explored these issues related to human relationships.

This book introduced the concept that behaviors could be sorted into four types based on a person's perception of self. He labeled these types Dominance (D), Inducement (I), Submission (S), and Compliance (C), but never developed an assessment based on these ideas.

William Moulton Marston's Legacy

This psychologist had a fascinating life and a wide range of accomplishments—many of which seem totally unrelated, but all go back to how the mind works.

- He consulted with Universal Studios in the 1930s to apply the principles from his book Emotions of Normal People as they transitioned from over-the-top melodrama of silent films to the more human subtlety of talking pictures.
- He wrote some of history's first "self-help" books on such topics as popularity, courage, attitudes, and determination. These were mass-marketed to the public and created a new industry.
- He is the inventor of Wonder Woman and wrote the comic book until his death in 1947. Her heroic behaviors draw much from his psychological writings. Harkening back to his early work with the lie detector, one of her greatest powers is using a "golden lasso of truth." He said about creating the character: "Not even girls want to be girls so long as our feminine archetype lacks force, strength and power. Not wanting to be girls, they don't want to be tender, submissive, peace-loving as good women are. Women's strong qualities have become despised because of their weakness. The obvious remedy is to create a feminine character with all the strength of Superman plus all the allure of a good and beautiful woman."

In the 1940s, industrial psychologist Walter V. Clarke built on Marston's theories to create an assessment instrument—or personality profile test—to aid businesses in hiring personnel. In 1956, he published it as a checklist called Activity Vector Analysis. In the 1960s, he worked with John Cleaver to create a new version of the assessment that would require respondents to choose between two or more terms. It wasn't until the 1990s that versions of this were published for individuals to do their own personality assessments for personal use.

The test has been updated over the years and continues to evolve. It is now a seventy-nine question assessment that asks respondents to indicate on a five-point scale how much each adjective describes them. The initials have shifted and now stand for Dominance (D), Influence (I), Steadiness (S), and Conscientiousness (C).

Dominance: direct, strong-willed, and forceful
Influence: sociable, talkative, and lively
Steadiness: gentle, accommodating, and soft-hearted
Conscientiousness: private, analytical, and logical

Although all people have some elements of each factor, most people tend toward one or two.

Even though the basic principles are tried and true, it is important to consider that there are many different versions of the DiSC profiles out there. Not only are there paper-and-pencil versus online versions, but slightly different variations on the test material as well. Not all are equally valid, and you should carefully evaluate whichever version you decide to use. You want to find one with the highest statistical correlation that measures not only the highest and lowest choices, but the rankings of all the adjectives. Remember, if you aren't sure, it would be best to work with a professional to give you the highest quality feedback.

Does This Pigeonhole People?

You may have heard criticisms of four-quadrant personality tests that they are pigeonholing or limiting people. It is important to remember that not everyone in a particular category will respond or act in the same way. We are all really a mix of all the dimensions, and each person is unique. These characterizations are not meant to restrict anyone to one thing, but to help understand how different people approach the world.

All the styles are equally valuable and there are successful people in each. As you do your assessments, you will need to decide what styles will be more relevant to your particular job opening. Salespeople often show up in the I quadrant, but that isn't to say that is the only one where they will be successful. This is why all three individual assessments are needed.

Application

- Don't just rely on one test and call it a day. These tests work best when they cover multiple aspects at once.
- Find a high-quality DiSC profile to start to understand each applicant's personality type.
- These assessments can be completed in-house, but you will get more accurate results by working with an expert consultant.

Chapter 4

Values and Motivators

The values and motivators component measures a person's driving factors. These questions help to unlock each person's "why"—what is truly important to them and how that directs their actions. Not only that, it explores the values and ethics that determine how an employee will behave.

For example, if a potential employee has a love of learning and a deep intellectual curiosity, they may not be satisfied with work on an assembly line, because it will prove too repetitive and boring. If a person responds that they give a lot of time and resources to charity or nonprofit work, they will likely be motivated by a genuine desire to help other people.

This type of test also indicates the ethics of an individual. Do they feel that rules or policies are for their safety and benefit, or do they think that rules can be broken when the end justifies the means? These different attitudes will affect employee behavior and understanding those values will help to manage and place employees in the optimal situations.

Why is this useful? Say you are considering a candidate for a leadership position. This portion of the test measures whether the candidate is assertive and wants to be visible, or whether they tend to prefer being "under-the-radar" and less visible. You know the team involved and that a present, dominant leader is needed to guide that team to success. The test results show you that a candidate has a low leadership visibility score—despite all their other qualifications, this candidate will not be a good fit.

This can save months of wasted energy wondering why the team is not responding to this leader's form of leadership.

Values Index—The Why of Human Performance

While there are several assessments that measure values, our system is based on research by Dr. Eduard Spranger and Dr. Gordon Allport. The values index is based around seven core dimensions that play a vital role in how we see the world and react to it. The attribute index is meant to help the respondent understand how they reason and make judgments or decisions.

Motivators are harder to determine without the help of assessments because they are below the surface, unlike the more observable personality traits discussed in the previous chapter. Your values are formed by your experiences and exposure to the world at large. A person's individual experiences related to each of seven core dimensions determine what they consider valuable or not. Positive and negative experiences will shape which values are given more weight. By the time one is an adult, these value dimensions are fairly set, though they can shift a bit over time. Overall, though, they are considered to be mostly static in the absence of a major life-changing event or crisis that can majorly disrupt set values.

Building a Complete Values Index

Dr. Eduard Spranger's research and observations led to the identification of six core attitudes or values he found present in every person. These six values were what he believed created motivation and drive in an individual. He defined them as, "world views or filters that shape and define that which a person finds valuable, important, good or desirous."

In the 1950s, American psychologist Dr. Gordon Allport picked up the mantle left by Dr. Spranger and became one of the first psychologists to really focus on personality in the United States. He rejected both Freud's psychoanalytic approach to personality, which he thought went too deep, and Marston's (creator of the DiSC) behavioral approach, which he felt did not go deep enough. He placed the most importance on the uniqueness of each individual, and the importance of the present context, as opposed to past history, for understanding the personality.

Allport believed that an individual's personality is largely founded upon people's values, or basic convictions that they hold about what is and is not of real importance in life. From this assumption, he began to work off of Spranger's findings outlining six major value types.

Working from Spranger's model, Allport and his two partners created the first values instrument to allow for measuring a person's value hierarchy (the Allport Vernon Lindzey Study of Values, 1956). In so doing, Allport replaced Spranger's original Political dimension with the Individualistic dimension, which he felt was more accurate. It is important to note that this was more than simply a name change. The Individualistic dimension is its own dimension, separate and discrete, from the Political dimension hypothesized by Spranger. Allport took the original Political dimension out and inserted the Individualistic dimension in its place.[1]

[1] Quoted from IMX Technical Manual, Innermetrix Inc. 2009. Peter T. Klassen, PhD, Leon Pomeroy PhD. and Robert S. Hartman PhD.

Spranger and Allport had different opinions on what had the greatest influence on each person's value hierarchy. Spranger felt that genetics played the most important role, while Allport believed that the socioeconomic experiences of one's childhood had more influence. Modern researchers think it is a mix of the two ideas: each person has a genetic predisposition toward certain traits or tendencies, but these are influenced by the environmental conditions of a person's life.

Seven Dimensions of Value

Both Spranger's and Allport's work—each having merit—needn't be mutually exclusive, which is why we use seven dimensions instead of six to capture all the dimensions of value. These are:

1. **Aesthetic**—A drive for balance, harmony, and form
2. **Altruistic**—A drive for humanitarian efforts or to help others altruistically
3. **Economic**—A drive for economic or practical returns
4. **Individualistic**—A drive to stand out as independent and unique
5. **Political**—A drive to be in control or have influence
6. **Regulatory**—A drive to establish order, routine and structure
7. **Theoretical**—A drive for knowledge, learning and understanding.

Each person has values associated with each of these core dimensions, but each person's distribution amongst the values is unique.

The assessment will not only indicate which dimensions are valued most highly, but also the degree to which they are valued. The level of motivation related to each dimension is a helpful indicator of how important something is in a person's life and is useful in understanding how it can benefit them.

A person's two highest ranked dimensions are the most inspiring to them and therefore should be highly connected to their work and life. The middle three dimensions are somewhat motivational but for the most part will be on par with the average population. The lowest two are more important than the middle three because these negative values can actually serve to "demotivate." Certain motivators will be excellent predictors of consistent high performance. As you evaluate potential candidates, you will want to be sure that their top and bottom motivating factors align with the position and environment of your organization.

The "why" of human performance is a major part of the equation, and when properly understood and implemented, can assist with workplace engagement and overall satisfaction. The lack of motivation and fulfillment in the workplace is a well-documented problem in modern society. Understanding what will drive your employees will help you match new hires with the work that resonates for them and allow you to more effectively lead them.

The next chapter discusses the final component in these assessments: Innate Talent.

Application

- Values and motivations will tell you a lot about what a person is best suited for. Use an instrument that gets to a person's "why."

Use these motivations to create a work environment that resonates and fulfills your employees.

Chapter 5
Select Those Hardwired for Success

The final component is an assessment to understand a person's innate talents—the sort of natural abilities that you are born with. This is based on the work of Dr. Robert Hartman, a German logician and philosopher, and Jay Niblick, a professional consultant who is an expert at applying Hartman's principles of axiology in a business environment.

Dr. Robert Hartman's primary area of study was axiology, the study of value. His lifelong quest was to answer the question, "What is good?" He formally defined value theory, based on three kinds of value: 1) intrinsic goods (i.e., people as ends in themselves); 2) extrinsic goods (i.e., things and actions as means to ends); and 3) systemic goods (conceptual values). Essentially, he felt all good things share a common formal or structural pattern, but that all good things are not equal. Therefore "how" we value is just as important as "what" we value. His work was considered revolutionary, and he was even nominated for the Nobel Peace Prize for his work in 1973, but he died that year before the awards, and it is never given posthumously.

Inspired by Hartman's work, Jay Niblick and his team embarked on a study, called The Genius Project, of highly successful people in a variety of industries, to try to understand if there was something that set them apart.

In his book, What's Your Genius?[1], he reports that they expected to find a common thread—perhaps a particular set of abilities that spelled success—but what they discovered surprised them.

What linked these geniuses was not a particular innate talent that is common to all successful individuals—it was that they were able to find roles that allowed them to use their unique talents effectively. Additionally, the study found that all successful people had two acquired skills (different from innate talents): self-awareness and authenticity. These may not seem like acquired skills, but they can certainly be learned. Self-awareness of your own talents and how to avoid your blind spots will help you maximize your potential. That is where the authenticity comes in—you must be true to yourself and not try to make yourself into something you are not.

> "The problem, though, is that the vast majority of people assume there is no real difference between talents and skills. They assume that natural talents can be developed through learning, training, and hard work. They fail to appreciate just how fixed the neural networks that control these talents really are. Instead, because they fail to differentiate between talents and skills, and because they assume that both can be acquired equally, they set about identifying what talents and skills they need for a given role and then start trying to develop them both...People exert a tremendous amount of energy attempting to change themselves in a way that just isn't going to lead to success, when in reality it is the outside world that needs to be changed. That's what geniuses do, they change the world in which their natural talents play."
>
> –Jay Niblick, What's Your Genius?

---

[1] Jay, Niblick. What's Your Genius How the Best Think for Success. Cork: BookBaby, 2010.

In an earlier chapter, I discussed that most training is not effective. That goes back to this difference between talents and skills. If a person already has the innate talents that make them a great salesperson, then training and acquiring skills in that area will only improve their success. However, a person can get all the training they can and maybe marginally improve, but without the background talents, they will never truly excel. By identifying what talents align with the job you are hiring for, you can find the candidates who are hardwired for success.

Find the Innate Talents You Need

First of all, you must evaluate the job you are hiring for and determine which of the areas of natural talent will best serve that position. Natural talents fit into three categories, or "classes of talent," based on Hartman and Niblick's categorizations. (The following descriptions are quoted from What's Your Genius?)

- The Head (Hartman's Systemic): the class of talents that deals with intellectual or conceptual thinking, creating order and structure, long-range planning, problem solving, and big-picture or strategic thinking. This class of talents is sometimes referred to as Thinking.
- The Hand (Hartman's Extrinsic): the class of talents that deals with practical thinking, real-world action orientation, details, results, and tangible or tactical thinking. This class of talents is sometimes referred to as Doing.
- The Heart (Hartman's Intrinsic): the class of talents that deals with people, empathy, sensitivity, and understanding for others, and emotional or humanistic thinking. Sometimes this class of talents is known as Feeling.

We all possess some ability in each of these areas, but what makes each person unique is which areas are more dominate and the particular combination. If someone is strong in one area, but in a position that requires more from their weaker areas, then they will constantly be fighting their own inner nature.

True Stories

Years ago I worked with a man named Tom Brown, a divisional president of United Water. Tom is a servant leader with the admiration and respect of his colleagues because he treats people well.

Tom had a big problem: a 40-million-dollar contract was in jeopardy of being lost and bid out because two consecutive hires for a key leadership role were not the right fit, and it made the client lose all confidence in their organization.

I helped Tom facilitate a two-day off-site meeting between the client company and the contract people that were working on-site at this facility to articulate what the issues were and how we might solve them. I also asked what the ideal characteristics of the new leader would be and set to work finding the ideal person to take over the project. Through targeted searching and applying the assessments, I was able to find a candidate with the right innate talents to excel in the position. We were able to salvage that contract from going to the competition, and they continue to be a long-term happy customer.

Think Outside the Box

The innate strengths assessment sometimes requires some creative interpretation. Perhaps a candidate has the right personality type and strong alignment with your values, but their particular combination of strengths doesn't seem as ideally suited to the position you have available.

Perhaps you are fitting the person to the job too much in this case. The job description is really just a guideline for achieving a goal that the company wants reached. Would there be another way of approaching the same goals that might better fit the candidate's talents and abilities?

> "What's a genius? Why, you're a genius. For a genius is nothing but a person who can put all his power into one thought."
>
> – Dr. Robert Hartman

Application

- Test for a person's hardwired talents and abilities—these are different from skills which can be learned over time.
- Look at the job and decide which strengths will best align with the type of job you are looking to fill.
- Don't be too literal—if there is a candidate that meets your other requirements but doesn't have the innate talents you had in mind, is there a way to meet the goals of the job in a way that works better for them?

Chapter 6

Interview Only Top Performers—Check for Chemistry, Culture, and Commitment

The assessment is a powerful tool for identifying top performers. But it is important to understand this fact: not all high performers are right for you. That may sound strange—why wouldn't you want all the brightest and best out there? Never underestimate the importance of chemistry.

In my experience, you should place about 80 percent of your hiring decision on the data from the assessment. This is an excellent indicator of future performance and you will know that the candidate is capable of performing the job. But the last 20 percent is all about the cultural fit—will this candidate be a good fit for your team and are they in alignment with your company values?

In this chapter, we'll discuss how you can use the interview to your best advantage.

"Setting the bar high in our approach to hiring has been, and will continue to be, the single most important element of [our] success."

– Jeff Bezos, Amazon

Identifying Top Performers

The best or most accurate way to identify new, high-potential, consistent top performers is to compare all applicant profile scores against the top 10 percent of current top performers in that given role. We have evaluated thousands of top performers in every role for residential real estate to know with certainty what the unique nuances or configuration of personality, motivators and talents look like. By using this proven science and comparison to the ideal hiring benchmarks for each position, we eliminate the costly, frustrating guesswork and consistently quadruple hiring success. All of this is done digitally for you.

Do you know the primary difference between a Buyer Agent and Listing Agent? A Listing Agent has a much higher sense of urgency. They are more about the "thrill of the hunt" or more transactional and less about building relationship and spending quality time with people. Using DiSC terminology they are much higher D's. A high D will not be the best personality style for working with buyers because a high D has a tendency to be much more impatient. Spending the weekend or longer with a couple who are indecisive would be difficult for them to self-manage. Inside they are screaming "get me out of here." The result is not instantaneous enough for a high D. In contrast, the ideal D score for a Buyer Agent is below 50 or on the lower to moderate side. Having a person with a D score of 25 as a Listing Agent would not be a good fit. The lower D has far less drive, urgency and pace and therefore will not deliver the volume of listings you desire.

The beauty of the three-part assessment is that you no longer have to waste time poring over resumes, looking for someone who might be the right fit. This data will give you the information you need to proceed. The point of these assessments is to identify who the high performers are before you even meet with them.

It is very important for this to be done before the interview takes place. Otherwise you risk wasting everyone's time if the assessments reveal the candidate was not among the high performers.

True Stories

Josh Roy is a very personable leader who cares about his people. Through sheer persistence, initiative, and drive, his residential real estate company succeeded and was recently ranked in Real Trends by The Wall Street Journal as one of the top 250 real estate firms in the United States.

He had a high-performing team of about fifteen employees, but his dilemma was it took him seventeen years of trial-and-error to build that team. He was spending a tremendous amount of time, effort, and resources hiring the wrong people.

Working with our firm and utilizing the scientific assessments, he was able to eliminate that trial-and-error. In our first year working with him, he was able to hire three significant peak performers that helped his company immeasurably.

The first hire was a sorely needed office manager. This person was such a good fit that Josh decided to proactively give her a raise after just eight months on the job, which was totally unprecedented in his company. The next employee was an inside salesperson who turned out to have performance double and triple the industry standard. The third hire was a listing agent, who in the first year became the number one salesperson on his team.

These successful hires have given Josh a new confidence, and he has expanded the vision for his business. He is now going to open ten additional offices expanding his operation tenfold.

Identify Your Corporate Culture

As you look to hire new candidates, take some time to understand your own company culture and values so you can better see how a potential employee will stack up. The assessment helps you to "hire fast," but now is the time to slow down a little to get it right. Taking the time to evaluate the fit will pay off as you bring them onboard later.

Corporate Culture refers to the beliefs and behaviors that determine how employees of a particular company interact and conduct business. Usually this has developed organically over time, and in most cases, culture is implied but not strictly defined. However, if you don't have a strong grasp on your own corporate culture, it would be beneficial to take a moment to evaluate it so you can better articulate it to candidates. Take a look at the company mission statement and have conversations with employees and clients. Think about how you truly behave and react to different scenarios; sometimes the aspirations of your mission statement do not really match up to reality.

Start with these questions to help you identify your company culture:

- What are some words or short phrases that would describe the company's atmosphere?
- What values are important to our company?
- What is central to the organization that should never change?
- How would we describe the working environment?
- What is the communication style of our company? Verbal or written? Direct or indirect?
- What are our meetings like? Serious? Casual? Highly structured or loose?
- Do we work collaboratively or independently?

- What types of employees do well here?
- How do we reward people who do well? What about if they don't do well?
- What makes our organization different from its competitors?
- What would clients or customers say about working with our company?
- Is this a friendly and informal atmosphere or is it formal and buttoned up?
- How many hours a week are people expected to work?
- Do employees socialize throughout the workday or after work?
- If we are recruiting for a particular team or department, what values or behaviors are specific to that team?

Sometimes this exercise is difficult to complete because you may feel too close to properly evaluate the culture. Or maybe your employees feel uncomfortable and won't give you entirely honest answers. In these circumstances, it would be wise to bring in a third party to help you evaluate, particularly one with expertise in organizational culture or staffing.

Start with Values

Before you have even interviewed a candidate, you will have some information about what each candidate finds important, since values and motivations are part of the assessments. In some cases, you may be able to eliminate some potential candidates altogether before they come in. For example, if your company values honesty and transparency, but the assessment reveals that a candidate has a low score for "attitude toward honesty," they may not be the best fit for you.

Use the values and talent assessment as a baseline for your discussions during the interviews to evaluate how well the candidates are aligned with the company values.

If the results indicate that someone values a "sense of belonging" and "personal relationships" they probably need to be part of a close and connected team. If that is what you have, then you should explore that in the interview. If your group tends to be independent and work on their own, this candidate may be unhappy there.

On the other hand, remember that you may not be looking for someone who is an exact replica of the other people in the organization. Adding people who have different outlooks gives your team diversity and balance. But if the core values of your organization don't line up with the candidate's, it will most likely be a poor match.

Work Commitment

Another area that needs to fit with your company culture is the level of commitment and time spent at work. You should have evaluated this when thinking about your own company culture so you have a good grasp on what you are expecting from employees. If you are not sure, here are a few more questions to think about:

- How many hours a week do you expect employees to work on average?
- Do you provide flexible work schedules or allow for telecommuting, or do you prefer people to work set hours?
- How much travel do you expect in this position?
- Are you looking for someone who will be here for a certain number of years, or as part of a succession plan for senior management?

Having these aspects be part of the discussion early on in the process will save a lot of trouble down the road. If your company has no intention to provide any flexible time or telecommuting options, that should be very clear from the initial discussions, because it may be a big downside for a potential employee leading to the wrong fit.

What Questions Should You Ask?

The value of the assessments will be very apparent as you prepare interview questions. In most job interviews, you are attempting to find out if a candidate can do the job. Maybe they have job experience in a similar position on their resume, but have they been successful in the past? With the data from the assessment you don't need to ask if they can do the job—you know they can.

Instead, you should be looking for cultural fit based on the ideas you have brainstormed above. This isn't always so easy to find out, but here are some questions you could ask to try to get a feel for how they would blend into your team.

1. Why do you want to work for this company, and what are your expectations? (A good way to find out if your values align with the candidate's.)

2. What's the greatest workday of your life? (This gives you an insight into what motivates them, and if that doesn't align with your company's "purpose," it probably won't be a great fit.)

3. What is teamwork to you? (Try doing this in front of the other people who would actually be on the candidate's team.)

4. What is one thing you believe that most people do not? (This is a favorite of Peter Thiel, founder of PayPal, because it gauges independent and creative thinking.)

5. Who inspires you and why? (You can learn a lot from who a person admires or looks up to.)

6. What was the best way you delegated a task? (In other words, are you leadership material?)

7. What are you passionate about? (If their passions don't align with your mission, then they might not be a good fit.)

8. What was a time you didn't know how to do something, and how did you handle it? (This provides insight into their problem-solving capabilities.)

9. What personality traits do you butt heads with? (This might reveal some potential conflicts in your group.)

10. What is your superpower? (Everyone is great at something, and this will help you ensure they are in the right role in your team.)

11. How do you rely on others to make you better? (As we discussed in chapter 6, self-awareness is a crucial quality, and if someone can discuss their weaknesses or blind spots with honesty, they will likely fit your team better than someone who isn't tuned into that.)

12. How would your coworkers describe your role on a team? (This makes them look at how others perceived them in past environments.)

13. What is your preferred relationship with people you work with? (This will give you a better idea of how they will fit your particular organization's style regarding coworkers.)

Test Them Out

Sometimes the most valuable way to see if a candidate would fit with the culture of your team is to do a trial run. Ask the candidate to come spend the day with you and the department, hopefully doing some of the actual work that this position would entail. The interview was a great opportunity to discuss the job with the potential employee, but since it is only an hour or so, most people can keep up a façade for the whole time. If they come to spend a day, especially if put into real scenarios, they are more likely to show their true self.

Observe carefully how they interact with the other employees. Do they work well with your systems and fit into the overall dynamic? Is there any tension with particular team members? Do they seem guarded or open to getting to know the other employees?

Don't forget to look for the little things that are part of company culture:

- Do they seem very neat or very messy?
- Do they have a good sense of humor?
- Are they aggressive or laid back? Does their attitude match the team?
- Are they consistent with how they represented themselves in the interview?

This really is a crucial part of the hiring process. All the skills in the world are not going to be helpful if an employee is in constant friction with the rest of the team. Taking the time to evaluate will be well worth it in the long run.

True Story

Mark Adams is the managing director at Vitsoe, the worldwide licensee of Dieter Ram's furniture collection, and he knows the power of being very selective in finding the right cultural fit. In addition to multiple interviews, they always have potential candidates work with them on an actual project to see how they work with the team. It is a nice way to evaluate the candidate in a very natural way, and everyone understands that no commitments have been made.

Mark told the Harvard Business Review[1] a story of a recent candidate who worked with the team on a shelf installation. This candidate was very adept at the skills of the job but the team noticed something at the end of the day: he threw his tools into the box when he was done instead of carefully putting them away. In discussions with the CEO, everyone agreed that this was a reason to not hire him.

Does that strike you as overly picky? Well, isn't that the point? Your selection criteria should be very specific to you—so much so that the wrong people shouldn't want to work for you. Getting fit right the first time is so important that Mark says he would rather be shorthanded than hire the wrong person.

---

[1] https://hbr.org/2014/03/hire-slow-fire-fast

Application

- Spend some time articulating your company culture so you can communicate it to potential employees.
- Use your values assessment to eliminate red flags and guide discussions with candidates.
- Don't forget the culture of working hours and commitment—does the candidate's drive match your organization? (Once I had a candidate withdraw herself because the team valued learning and read a book every quarter together; however, the potential new hire hated reading and asked to be removed from consideration.)
- Test them out by having a day onsite with their potential coworkers and work tasks. Observe them carefully during this time.

Section III

After You Hire Fast, What Comes Next?

Chapter 7
Accelerate Onboarding

You had all the information you needed to choose the right candidate. You narrowed down those hardwired for success and brought them in to evaluate how they will fit your team. You made the offer and it was accepted. Now what?

The first weeks for a new hire are crucial to setting them up for success. You can't just throw the person in and hope for the best. Even if they have the innate talents to thrive, you can vastly improve the situation depending on how they are introduced to the company. The term "onboarding" has become popular to describe the ways new employees acquire the necessary knowledge, skills, and corporate culture to become effective team members. Think beyond just a simple new-employee orientation. Organizations with a strong onboarding process improve new hire retention by 82 percent and productivity by over 70 percent (The True Cost of a Bad Hire, Bandon Hall).

Tell Them Why They Were Hired

The basic human resources orientation to a new company usually includes lots of paperwork, navigation of new spaces, and introductions. A new employee certainly will know where the paper clips are stored and who to contact about their 401K contributions, but will they have all they need to succeed in this position? Probably not.

The good news is, because of the hiring process this book describes, you have vast amounts of information at the ready about the new employee and how they work at their best. You can use this to your advantage by sharing it with the new hire. Tell them exactly why they were hired. This doesn't sound that revolutionary, but think about it—has that ever happened to you when you started a new job? Wouldn't it be encouraging to know that you were someone that was in the top 10 percent in terms of potential for success? I have done this thousands of times and not one person has ever experienced anything like this. They are amazed.

As a leader, you should set up a meeting with the new employee as soon as possible, at least within the first week. The primary purpose of this meeting is to uplift, to affirm, to encourage, to support, to emphasize that you believe in them. Tell them that based on the assessments, it is not a matter of if they can be successful, but how successful, because you know they have what it takes to be a consistent top performer.

This will be a massive encouragement to the new hire and an affirmation that they made a great decision in joining your team. Speaking of leadership, one in two employees left a job because of their manager, according to a survey measuring the engagement of 27 million employees ("State of the American Manager," Gallup).

Using the assessments, you can create a strength plan to summarize the data and elaborate on three components:

1. **Communication Style**: How do they prefer to be communicated with? This is vital to success within the team and it is vital for you and the new hire to be on the same page right away.

2. **Motivations**: A review of what drives the new employee provides deep insight into how to create the ideal work environment.

3. **Innate Talents:** What are the strengths they should focus on and what should be taken off their plate?

Craft the Job to the Employee

The strengths plan is a great way for you to set expectations with the new hire about their goals and to determine how they can be set up to fulfill their potential. With the information from the assessments, you can craft the job to fit the style of this specific employee. You shouldn't have a one-size-fits-all leadership style. Remember that you have chosen this person because of their individual qualities, so don't then try to fit them into the box of the job description.

Clear communication will be a major element in the ultimate success of an employee. Some people prefer verbal communications while others want everything in writing. Some might like things to be one-on-one, while others would like a group discussion. Try to approach your employee the way they prefer so they are not frustrated by your communications with them.

Knowing the motivations or what drives your employees enables you to make a significant impact on how to best lead and engage them. From my leadership consulting days, the leadership definition I use the most is, "Leadership is creating the conditions that focus and enlists the talents and energy of others towards the stated goals of the organization."

To illustrate: if a person values autonomy and freedom the most, support them when they ask for help but otherwise stay out of their way. If you try to micromanage an employee like that, he or she will quickly become frustrated and start to look elsewhere. A consultant named Rich Schlentz provides a definition of engagement that we as leaders should all aspire to attain.

"Engagement is the ability to capture people's souls, hearts and minds instilling an intrinsic passion for excellence and action." Engaging existing employees to their fullest extent by creating the best work environment and selecting new hires according to the ideal motivators, innate talents, and personality is a massive game changer when it comes to elevating performance. Inc. revealed "The Holy Grail in business today is engagement: employees' energy, enthusiasm and commitment to their companies. Engagement has a powerful effect not only on productivity but also on profitability and customer metrics, numerous studies show."[1]

The innate talents you discovered in the assessments will help you suit the individual elements of the job to the employee. The tasks that work with their innate strengths will be easy and enjoyable, but those that work against them will be a constant drain. Let me give you an example. An employee who is a phenomenal, gifted, persuasive, compelling communicator should not be doing administrative paperwork.

They are not good at it, and it saps them of all their energy because they know they are not good at it. That type of person needs somebody supporting them to handle the administrative stuff so that they can spend more of their time in the high-value, high-return category of what they do best: qualifying and closing more deals. Conversely, if someone has major analytical strengths, don't force them to spend a lot of energy giving presentations.

One check-printing company I worked with had two managers with opposite strengths and talents. One manager was gifted at operational details but hated public speaking and was petrified to get up in front of people at team meetings. The other manager loved being the center of attention and really shined when communicating with the team, but was hopeless with administrative tasks.

Rather than both of them struggling, we came up with the solution to allow them to share responsibilities so they could operate in their areas of comfort and both shine. The first manager monitored the payroll, vacation scheduling, and other minutiae for both teams, and the second handled the communications and presentations.

This unorthodox situation allowed both to succeed at a higher level in their main job functions without being bogged down with things that drained and frustrated them. Obviously in each of these cases, there will be times where things can't be precisely suited to every employee every time. Maybe the CEO has a roundtable meeting every month that just can't be avoided, even if an employee hates group discussions. Maybe there are paperwork or presentations that just have to be done by everyone from time to time.

But, if the jobs are adapted appropriately to suit the employee's innate strengths and motivations, they will be able to operate at their highest levels the majority of the time. Let's take a brief look at how the global workforce is doing in this area.

Each year, IBM conducts a global study and interviews over 1,000 CEOs. The following is from their 2015 report. "Only 11 percent of employees worldwide are engaged in their jobs according to Gallup. That's an amazingly low number and suggests profound problems for workplaces in almost every corner of the world.

Low engagement results in lower productivity and profitability and damages a company's future prosperity...one significant, tangible way to boost engagement is to help employees know their strengths." Talent expert Lynda Ross-Vega puts it this way: "Success in everything you do starts with the inner game—knowing who you are, what you do best and putting that knowledge to work for you."

Helping both your existing employees understand their strengths and assessing each person's talents, motivators. and personality style is perhaps the single best solution and opportunity to dramatically elevate your organization's performance. Here is just one of many compelling examples.

Furnitureland South (FLS) is the world's largest retail furniture showroom with more than 1.3 million square feet of floor space. With twenty-three football fields of furniture all in the same location, it is easy to be overwhelmed with the massive selection. During the 1990s, annual sales increased from $20 million to $129 million, and by 2004 their revenue reached $180 million.

Prior to my starting to work with FLS, they had experienced seven consecutive years of negative sales, had a 55 percent sales turnover rate, and all seven competitors around them went out of business—it was now late 2010. In my first thirty days working with FLS, they experienced an unprecedented 48 percent sales growth.

Since the economy was so weak at that point and there was a shortage of success stories in the marketplace, when CBS Evening News heard about the incredible achievement, they promptly made arrangements to fly one of their camera crews onsite. In early December, FLS was featured on CBS Evening News with Katie Couric as the lead story. And yet, retail furniture, the industry segment whose sales had fallen the farthest the fastest and was not expected to recover, had experienced exceptional sales growth.

How? The first thing I did was to evaluate all 150 straight-commission design consultants and the sales leaders with the three-part profiles—personality, motivators, and talents.

Second, I created a one-page executive summary, or what I call a "strength plan," from the seventy pages of data that primarily covers how to: best communicate with them according to their personality style; create the ideal work environment by catering to what motivates and drives them; and leverage their strengths, not play to their deficiencies, as well as reveal any blind spots or areas of opportunity.

Third, I met with each individual one-on-one, to collaborate on their strength plan and make any appropriate changes. The primary purpose for meeting was to elevate their self-awareness to give them the best opportunity to improve their performance and to uplift, encourage, and affirm each person by focusing on what is great about them.

After seven years of negative sales, the sales force was one of the most discouraged I had ever encountered. Not only were they working harder and making less money (struggling due to the recession), there were significantly fewer potential buyers visiting the store as well. Some of the better salespeople had seen their incomes cut in half, while others fared even worse.

Since I was the first outside consultant to be hired in the 47-year history of the company, it was natural for the salespeople to think, "who are you, do I like you, do I trust you, what is the reason you are really here, and is my job safe?" Due to these variables, the stakes were especially high for the first few one-on-one meetings to go well; these would either be my biggest advocates or detractors.

Based on my approach and style and the purpose of the one-on-ones, it is virtually impossible for participants to have a poor experience. The design consultants came out of the one-on-ones encouraged and energized and were zealots to the rest of their peers about their experience.

In order to leverage the value of these strength plans to their fullest extent, I then met with all of the sales leaders and went over each of their salespeople's strength plans to empower the leadership team. Shortly afterwards, the sales leaders met with each of their people for the purpose of comparing each other's strength plans and sharing any personal insights from the experience.

The next phase of the initiative was to eliminate their costly 55 percent sales turnover. To do this, the first step was to create a normative pattern, or benchmark of the assessment scores of the top twenty salespeople. This is the data that all potential new hires would be compared against. If a candidate's score were either similar to or better than the top twenty salespeople, we interviewed them.

If their scores were lower than the top twenty, then we passed on them—we did not interview them. By using this time-tested, scientifically proven approach to hiring we eliminated their 55 percent sales turnover completely. Not one straight commission sales and design consultant left the company for poor performance during my fifteen-month contract. There were two other very important components of the transformational sales results.

First, I delivered live sales keynotes. The emphasis was teaching the sales force "How to Sell Faster, Easier and Close More by Pushing the Buy Button in the Brain." The content focused on two critical areas: how to identify the different buyer styles, and personalizing your presentation/communication to how the client wants to buy. Since a person's personality style dictates how and why they buy as well as how they want you to communicate with them, being able to recognize a buyer's style is absolutely critical. Mastery of this sales content is without question the single most powerful and valuable in terms of impact.

In their book, Click: The Forces Behind How We Fully Engage with People, Work, and Everything We Do, the Brafman brothers say, "Clicking can be defined as an immediate, deep and meaningful connection with another person...we have to gain the other person's trust and he or she has to gain ours. We need to find a common language, understand each other's quirks and establish an emotional bond...sometimes this process is greatly accelerated and the connection seems to form almost magically and instantaneously...things feel right, we hit it off. There is an immediate sense of familiarity and comfort."[2]

Imagine your salespeople being able to connect and sell in this manner. The ABCs of selling are not the old-school, offensive "Always Be Closing;" instead, it is "Always Be Connecting." As Jeffrey Gitomer puts it: "Not being able to close is not a problem it is a symptom." Interestingly, the top twenty salespeople at FLS had an average increase in sales of almost 60 percent, while the remaining 130 salespeople had an increase of less than 10 percent. All 150 heard the same message at the same time.

The difference was the top twenty had a unique combination of personality style, motivators, and innate talents that were ideal for consistent, high performance in sales. The final piece of the high performance transformation was identifying the top ten sales objections and assembling volunteer task forces to secure the best thinking or best practices in order to craft the absolute best responses on how to eliminate those objections. For the sake of time, I will list just two common objections 1) "I'm just browsing," and 2) Eliminate price objections or buyer's negotiating. I will never forget one of the best yet very humble salespeople raising her hand to volunteer for #2. She prefaced volunteering by saying, "I am not sure if I am the best person to help with eliminating price objections.

Over the last twenty years I hardly ever have had anyone negotiate price with me." To sum up, when FLS retained me to help turn around their seven-year negative sales skid, in our first month we had a 48 percent sales growth and were featured on national television, we eliminated a 55 percent sales turnover and achieved sales growth for the first time in eight years.

Consider what Ken Robinson has to say: "Activities we love fill us with energy even when we are physically exhausted. Activities we don't like can drain us in minutes, even if we approach them at our physical peak of fitness. This is one of the keys to the Element and one of the primary reasons why finding the Element is vital for every person. When people place themselves in situations that lead to their being in the zone, they tap into a primal source of energy. They are literally more alive because of it.

In doing it they feel like their more authentic selves. They find that time passes differently and they are more alive, more centered and more vibrant than at any other times...takes them beyond the ordinary experiences of enjoyment and happiness...they connect with something fundamental to their sense of identity, purpose and well being.

Being there provides a sense of self-revelation, of defining who they really are and what they're really meant to be doing with their lives."[3] In their book entitled, The One Thing, authors Gary Keller and Jay Papasan say, "The one thing we must all understand if we are to achieve extraordinary results at our highest level possible. Undoubtedly. Unquestionably. Success is an inside job." I have been a zealot advocating this truth for more than two decades - it is refreshing knowing we now have a mountain of overwhelming evidence that makes this fact self-evident.

What About Inboarding?

The counterpart to "onboarding" for your current employees is known as "inboarding," and it can be a great way to regularly check in with and develop your team. I have already discussed that the assessments are a valuable tool, not just for hiring, but also for evaluating your current staff. The same process of assessments, discussions, and adaptations could be equally valuable for your employees who are already at the company. You may discover some surprising things.

There may be subtle shifts in job duties or motivations that will help your other employees function at a higher level. One of the biggest benefits of inboarding is the assessments will tell us how many of your employees are flight risks. We have saved countless people from leaving organizations by first of all having the insight something is wrong and then being intentional about having a transparent conversation with the employee about it.

This process may also reveal that you have some employees who are wildly unsuited to their current positions. This will most likely not be surprising—you most likely already see that they are struggling. Looking at the assessment results may help you to see a different position in the company that would be a better match to their innate talents. The employee may just shine in another area and become a much more valuable member of the organization.

But you may find that there are others that will simply never be successful in their positions or your company. All the training courses in the world will not change their innate strengths and they will constantly be swimming upstream. Robert Hartman puts it this way: "Stop trying to put in what God left out and instead work with what He put in." While it is never easy to fire someone, doing this quickly and humanely will be better for everyone involved.

It is not a kindness to drag the process out in the misguided hopes that they can "improve" when you can clearly see that they do not have the underlying attributes necessary.

But "fire fast" doesn't mean kick them out the door. Take the time to review the assessments with them so that they learn the valuable information about themselves that will help them to find the type of position that they can succeed at.

Though they may not be suited to sales, they may be an incredibly detail-oriented copyeditor or genius computer programmer. Give them the gift of insight into the type of work that will make them happy and successful.

Application

- Set up a meeting with a new hire to tell them why they were hired and why you think they are destined for success.
- Discuss the employee's communications style, motivations, and innate talents and how those will shape their new position.
- Adapt your leadership style to that employee for the best results.
- Try inboarding by giving the assessments to your current employees and discussing the results with them.
- Fire fast when necessary, but give them the tools to find the job they are really suited for.

---

[1] http://www.inc.com/magazine/201306/leigh-buchanan/traits-of-true-leaders.html

[2] Brafman, Ori, and Rom Brafman. Click: The Forces behind How We Fully Engage with People, Work, and Everything We Do. New York: Crown Business, 2010.

[3] Robinson, Ken, and Lou Aronica. The Element: How Finding Your Passion Changes Everything. New York: Viking, 2009.

Chapter 8
The Hire Fast Fire Fast Checklist

The main message of this book is as follows: when you implement a time-tested, scientifically proven hiring system, you take the subjectivity out and eliminate the costly, frustrating guesswork from your hiring process. After all, knowing is always better than guessing! Using assessments to identify the right candidates quickly, allows you to feel supremely confident about your hiring decisions. Perhaps the best part of quadrupling your hiring effectiveness is that it helps to ensure significant competitive advantage. As Steve Jobs once said, "A small team of A+ players can run circles around a giant team of B and C players."

There are certain innate abilities that people have and when they are in a position that aligns with their true nature, they are wildly successful. You can identify those qualities before you hire someone—and it can be done quickly and easily. Here is a handy checklist for the Hire Fast, Fire Fast System:

- Ask for help if you need it—recruiters can help take your search to the next level.
- Don't just rely on one test and call it a day. These tests work best when they cover multiple aspects at once.
- Find a high quality DiSC profile to start to understand each applicant's personality type.
- These assessments can be completed in-house, but you will get more accurate results by working with an expert consultant.

- Values and motivations will tell you a lot about what a person is best suited for. Use an instrument that gets to a person's "why."
- Use these motivations to create a work environment that resonates and fulfills your employees.
- Test for a person's hardwired talents and abilities—these are different from skills which can be learned over time.
- Look at the job and decide which strengths will best align with the type of job you are looking to fill.
- Don't be too literal—if there is a candidate that meets your other requirements but doesn't have the innate talents you had in mind, is there a way to meet the goals of the job in a way that works better for them?
- Spend some time articulating your company culture so you can communicate it to potential employees.
- Use your values assessment to eliminate red flags and guide discussions with candidates.
- Don't forget the culture of working hours and commitment—does the candidate's drive match your organization?
- Test them out by having a day onsite with their potential coworkers and work tasks. Observe them carefully during this time.
- Set up a meeting with a new hire to tell them why they were hired and why you think they are destined for success.
- Discuss the employee's communications style, motivations, and innate talents and how those will shape their new position.
- Adapt your leadership style to that employee for the best results.
- Try inboarding by giving the assessments to your current employees and discussing the results with them.
- Fire fast when necessary, but give them the tools to find the job they are really suited for.

John Pyke "The Talent Genius"

Final Thoughts

Stephen Covey once said, "If you want to make small improvements, change your behavior, but if you want to make quantum improvements, change your paradigm." Simply put, when you consistently hire people utilizing the accuracy and advanced insights of a set of comprehensive, time-tested, scientifically proven assessments (measuring innate talents, motivators, and personality style), you will experience a quantitative competitive advantage or quantum improvements.

To illustrate, "Recruiting is the HR function with the highest impact on revenue. Excellent recruiting practices contribute to more than 3X revenue growth and 2X profit margins" ("Realizing the Value of People Management," Gallup).

It has been said every company has two major challenges—sales and everything else. Sales are unquestionably the lifeblood of any business. As a result, hiring the best salespeople the first time, every time and building a world-class sales organization is one of the most important strategic imperatives for executive leadership.

In their book Mavericks at Work, William Taylor and Polly LaBarre state: "Leaders...understand that the only sustainable form of market leadership is thought leadership."[1] What I have shared with you is undeniable hiring truth and hiring thought leadership validated by a history of unmatched results. The days of doing the same things and expecting different results in business have given way to an incredible validated discovery that will transform your organization's results. Candidly, you have too much to gain to ignore it!

John Keats once said, "Nothing ever becomes real until it is experienced. Even a proverb is no proverb to you until your life has illustrated it." As such, I invite you to experience the power of these solutions firsthand. Contact me today for a free test drive. When it comes to hiring, consistent peak performance and ensuring sustainable, competitive advantage, you can confidently stop leaving it up to chance.

After all, knowing is always better than guessing, and moving risk as far away from you as possible is the name of the game. There is simply no substitute for making decisions and operating from statistically validated and scientifically proven numbers. In the words of the world's leading creativity and innovation expert, Edward de Bono, "The quality of our thinking will determine the quality of our future." Your best hiring and business results await you.

---

[1] Taylor, William, and Polly LaBarre G. Mavericks at Work: Why the Most Original Minds in Business Win. New York: William Morrow, 2006.

Section IV
Bonus Chapters – Important Considerations

Chapter 9

Differentiation – A Compelling, Unique Selling Proposition

What is it that makes you stand out in the marketplace? In other words, how are you different, better or unique? What do you offer that sets you apart and motivates both buyers and sellers to only want to work with you and your firm? What is it about your marketing, your messaging and your lead generation that would attract the best agents to join your team or make hiring superstars much easier? Simply put, what is your unique selling proposition (USP)? The purpose of this chapter is to provide one powerful example of perhaps the most compelling USP I have ever heard or experienced in order to encourage you to evaluate your own positioning in the marketplace.

As a sales expert I often deliver keynotes entitled, "How to Push the Buy Button in the Brain? Sell Faster, Easier and Trigger More Decisions in Your Favor." Recent research in the field of neuroscience indicates there is a buy button in the brain.

The premise is that you can push the buy button at any time with anyone to accelerate the sale, trigger more decisions in your favor and close more business. Although the brain is only 2% - 3% of our body mass, it consumes 25% of the body's energy. Interestingly, the brain is constantly scanning for contrast. The more contrast, the less energy the brain uses (the less thinking and analyzing occurs) and the more deciding occurs. Little or no contrast means little or no decisions in your favor. Let me give you an example of what I mean.

Due to a change in our plans, we listed a prime piece of residential property during the last recession. It was the largest lot in the subdivision at 2.4 acres, in the middle of the cul-de-sac, a stone's throw outside of town thereby property taxes were much lower and the location was within a ten minute drive to literally everything one needed. None of that mattered – selling property at a time when banks were dumping six figure lots nearby for twenty cents on the dollar and considering the custom home market was very sluggish made selling very difficult.

After years of virtually no interest, I heard Glenn Beck deliver a very compelling radio ad endorsing a local realtor I did not know. His name was Jason Bramblett from Jason Bramblett and Associates. The contrast and differentiation was so great I had one of those "I could've had a V8" moments and I called Jason immediately. Not only did Jason sell my property quickly, my loss on the property was minimal. Simply put, Jason's USP was so compelling and the contrast was so significant, it was the single strongest USP I have ever experienced.

Jason is part of an elite group of brokers partnering with a firm called Radio and Television Experts (RATE). Here is how it works. RATE uses a brilliant, proven marketing and messaging strategy sometimes called "standing on the shoulders of giants" or celebrity endorsements.

One of the biggest ways to stand out from all others and earn an unfair advantage of breaking through the wall of trust is having an authoritative voice or personality that the viewer or listener trusts, reassure them that you deserve their trust.

In my case that celebrity was Glenn Beck. Their most recent celebrity is Barbara Corcoran from Shark Tank who also was a successful real estate mogul in New York City.

To underscore the prominence of using celebrity endorsements, this past January, 38 different celebrities were used on TV commercials during the Super Bowl - the single annual event that showcases the best ads at the most expensive times of the year. In a recent article in the US Today, Frank Germann, a marketing professor at the University of Notre Dame, was quoted as saying "there is evidence that celebrities make a commercial more memorable..." and a key component is "how well that marriage was thought out - what the celebrity means to the brand."

In addition to the celebrity endorsements, part of the package often includes a guaranteed home sale program. If the home is not sold in a certain period of time, the broker purchases the home at a price agreed to beforehand. RATE's powerful, non-duplicatible marketing and lead generation system using celebrity endorsement not only provides a compelling USP, they also have an unmatched track record of consistently delivering high quality leads helping brokers earn millions of dollars in trackable GCI.

Another huge benefit of being part of the RATE family is masterminding with other top agents in the industry. RATE has the largest client base of the most successful real estate agents using radio and television advertising effectively and profitably. They also have a private forum where agents can share their successful systems and strategies as well as events where agents can learn from each other.

Since RATE offers market exclusivity, their clients are far more willing to share knowing their advantages will not be shared with their competition. The ability to associate with and learn from the most profitable and successful leaders in the industry has a massive impact on a broker's business and ultimately their life.

In my view, having a USP for agents as well as consumers is of equal importance. If you have a powerful USP but do not have the talent to qualify and close the quality leads your USP creates you do not have a sustainable, profitable business model.

As a result, what is it about your infrastructure, systems and policies would be appealing to attract the best talent? Do you have an inside sales team that helps quality leads and set appointments for your agents? How do you maximize their selling time so they spend most of their time doing what they do best – qualifying and closing more deals.

Do you minimize their administrative time knowing it zaps their energy since they struggle with paperwork? Be intentional about creating the most compelling opportunity for agents to make the most money in the shortest period of time and you will have no issues with engagement, performance or turnover.To summarize, take time to create a compelling USP for both your potential clients and for attracting the best talent.

Chapter 10
Get LinkedIn or Get Left Out

Are you LinkedIn or Missing Out? If you are anything like me, LinkedIn was likely on the bottom of your list for social media and networking sites or perhaps it did not even make the list at all? Less than 10% of all real estate agents use LinkedIn as part of their strategic branding and lead generation platform despite the fact that it is one of the absolute best ways to differentiate, establish credibility and form powerful relationships.

The real estate agents who use LinkedIn know it has transformed into an interactive, vibrant business community, more than doubling in size in the last two years. With a new member joining less than every two seconds, LinkedIn is growing faster than Facebook and Twitter combined. The fact that Microsoft recently purchased LinkedIn for over 26 billion dollars is another strong indication you need to make LinkedIn a top priority.

LinkedIn provides you with easy to use tools as well as a platform to publish, connect and develop relationships with prospects, clients and referral sources. Simply put, the reason to make LinkedIn a priority is due to it's potential to translate into significant business.

Most agents and other professionals do not understand the power of LinkedIn. Countless agents have joined LinkedIn as a result of receiving an invitation from a friend or colleague. In response, the majority put up a quick and dirty profile just like I did.

Rarely do people take the time to create a complete profile or better yet, have an expert transform it for them.

A small list of what LinkedIn provides is as follows:

- Credibility and branding online to share your background and experience
- A platform to create followers from content you publish
- An information goldmine to learn about prospects, clients, realtors and referral sources
- A place to build a list of followers
- A professional platform to create relationships with prospects and referral sources you might otherwise never meet
- A place to build an online community with groups - either joining or creating one
- A method to stay top of mind with your prospects, clients and referral partners
- A platform to showcase recommendations, awards, interests and causes you care about

One of the most important reasons to have an exceptional profile on LinkedIn is due to what Google said: "56% of the sales process happens before anyone ever contacts you." If you are on LinkedIn, it is likely your LinkedIn profile will show up on the first page of Google unless you have a common name like John Smith. When your profile comes up on Google, if you were to read it as someone who was interested in working with you, how would it impact your decision? My profile was an absolute embarrassment. In addition to only being 5% completed, it did not convey in a compelling manner who I am, what I do and why someone should work with me. Now, I have a world-class profile that is in alignment with and consistent with all the other investments I have made in marketing. A LinkedIn profile is your digital footprint leaving a lasting first impression. What does your LinkedIn profile tell visitors who want to learn more about you?

Some of the best reasons you need an amazing LinkedIn profile include:

- LinkedIn is a site where you can tell visitors who you are, why you are passionate about what you do, how you are different or better from your competition, share your interests and specialties as well as your education, awards you have won, articles you have written and include audio or video testimonials from your clients and referral partners.
- LinkedIn is an excellent place to join groups or start a group and become known as an expert in your field. Groups offer real estate agents the opportunity to network with professionals that can result in leads, deals and more. It Is a place to network with professionals who can refer business to you and to whom you can refer business. It is a place where you can establish yourself as an expert.
- LinkedIn is an ideal platform to create relationships with other professionals who can be referral partners such as divorce attorneys, mediators, CPA's, estate planning attorneys, mortgage professionals and other real estate professionals.
- LinkedIn allows you to obtain valuable information about your prospects, other realtors and clients. Since LinkedIn allows members to publish their interests, where they went to school, recommendations and more, it is an excellent source of information.
- LinkedIn allows you to publish both written as well as audio and video testimonials of clients and other professionals who work with you. This is far more powerful than a testimonial on a website because typically the person giving the recommendation will have a profile on LinkedIn that can be viewed which eliminates any questions about the validity of the recommendation.

- LinkedIn provides you an opportunity to learn about others in their industry and make strong connections with referral partners. Real estate agents who use LinkedIn to grow their business leverage the power of the "advanced search" feature.
- LinkedIn is an excellent resource for creating a community of recommended resources to provide to their clients.
- LinkedIn is a great way to develop a referral relationship with others that are in other states or countries. With a few clicks, relationships that might be geographically prohibited become accessible.
- LinkedIn can put you higher in the search engines

To understand the power of LinkedIn and how important a LinkedIn profile can be for you, I highly recommend you take some time to peruse some exceptional LinkedIn profiles. One of the profiles is mine. Please send me an invite and I will be sure to accept it. Here is the link:

https://www.linkedin.com/in/thetalentgenius.com

Following are two awesome LinkedIn profiles of top real estate brokers that tell visitors who they are, why someone should work with them or join their team and provide everything a prospect or referral partner would need to know about working with this person:

https://www.linkedin.com/in/wesmadden

https://www.linkedin.com/in/bradkorb
Some experts say if you do not have a presence on LinkedIn, you do not exist. With more than 380 million professionals worldwide, and a new member joining every two seconds, the opportunities for establishing credibility and connections are endless.

With more than 2.2 million groups to join, there is no shortage of new people to meet within your industry and ways to establish yourself as the "go to" expert in your community. If you are not on LinkedIn, you may be left out.

Having a strong LinkedIn presence can make a huge difference in your bottom line – it sure has positively impacted mine. That is why I am including this content as a bonus chapter. Remember, first impressions are lasting.

Take the time to develop a strong LinkedIn profile that highlights your skills, certifications, biographical information, video testimonials as well as anything you want your ideal client to know about you.

Keep in touch with your network on a consistent basis. If you do not have time or knowledge to make LinkedIn a priority, hire someone to do it for you. To receive Rhonda's Resources for Realtors – Take LinkedIn to the Top – send an email to LinkedIndiva@gmail.com. Phone number is 760-515-2822

Chapter 11

Coaching – Accelerate Your Learning and Success

There are many coaching voices in the real estate world willing to tell you the best way to be successful. My strong recommendation is for you to seek out the help of a quality coach or consulting firm. Roy H. Williams put it this way, "You need a consultant because you have a blind spot (If you knew what it was, they wouldn't call it a blind spot). You're on the inside looking out. It's hard to read the label when you're inside the bottle. Your consultant is on the outside looking in." As someone who has been in the training and development and consulting field for over twenty years, the value of the right coach and/or consultant cannot be overstated.

From my perspective there is one firm specializing in real estate that stands head and shoulders above all others. My opinion is based on the best and most reliable feedback of all – client feedback. Clients of Corcoran Coaching and Consulting consistently rave about the value they bring and the return on investment gained. There are very few coaches that will start by asking your definition of success.

What is it that you want? And what are you looking for in a coach? This personalized element is just one of many things that sets Corcoran Coaching and Consulting apart from other real estate coaching companies. They exist to promote your success, not theirs.

There are plenty of coaching companies that specialize in helping new agents or those stuck at 20 transactions a year, but there are very few coaching companies that can help you build a thriving real estate business that operates beyond simply making more phone calls, and transforms your group of agents into a well-organized, high-producing real estate team. Corcoran Coaching and Consulting are not interested in helping a real estate agent build a career, their aim is to help you as the CEO build a team.

They want to help you become the CEO of your business and build a thriving team. That's not a job description they have written in their vault. They help you write it. Again, the first question is about what you want. Do you want to be a competing broker? Do you want to be a managing broker? Do you want to run your office from a houseboat off the Atlantic coast? (Yes, they helped that guy). Or maybe you want out and realize there's no exit strategy in place. Whatever your answer is, they will help you lay out that plan, then work the steps to achieve the goal. Their relationship with you is simple, but deep.

With you as CEO, they come in as a sort of a Board of Directors, to encourage, empower, and guide you. From the very beginning, they take a holistic approach by working with every department in your organization: operations, support staff, sales, recruiting and interviewing, profit and loss statements, business planning, accountability, work-life balance and operational excellence. The single most coveted aspect I consistently hear from their clients is how much they value the accountability – someone who appropriately pushes them to be the best they can be. They have learned from years of experience that success isn't going to come from one area of your business operating efficiently.

Success happens when each part of the whole is working together toward a common goal, with unified purpose.

Many people ask them, "What is the difference between Consulting and Coaching?" The relationship between the two is organic, and will flow from one to the other throughout their relationship with your company. In short, consulting begins as they learn about your business - what works, what's broken, holes in the business plan or budget, challenges within your team. As consultants, they will examine your business from top to bottom.

Your coaching program will begin to take shape as they get a clear picture of your needs. This is where they open their toolbox and begin filling yours! Their systems are time-tested and proven. While they are constantly improving them and tailoring them for each individual client's needs, they also know that the foundational principles they are built on are trustworthy and effective. Lead generation and follow-up, operations, client communication...if you do it more than once, it should have a system.

Once they have established that the foundation of your business is on a sound infrastructure, they can begin to build multiple pillars on top of it. They don't want the entirety of your business based solely on your referrals. They will introduce other pillars - property management, new home construction, geographic expansion, first time home buyers, a mortgage company, title company - whatever will best fit your business and situation.

At Corcoran, they recognize genuine success is a marathon run, not a sprint. They are committed to going the distance and are prepared to work hard alongside you for your success. They recognize, though, that their efforts will only be as successful as your implementation.

Numbers are important. That's one of the first things they teach their clients. And within the first year of coaching, their average client has decreased expenses by 23% and increased production by 47%. Those are compelling numbers hence why their clients rave about them.

Did you realize that 83 of their clients were named among the top 250 real estate professionals in the country by the Wall Street Journal and Real Trends, winning a total of 102 awards. Yes, numbers are important, and those are some pretty good numbers - but they aren't the whole picture.

Remember, their goal is your success, by your definition. They also have a definition of success for themselves. They are here to help you balance success in business while building value in life. The achievement of work-life balance is one of the things they are most proud to accomplish with a client. You have the definition of what your success looks like. Helping you achieve this balanced, healthy, and productive approach to your life and business is the essence of Corcoran Coaching and Consulting.

Are you ready to begin this adventure? Contact them today.

Chapter 12

Wealth Mastery - Protect and Leverage Your Money

The following chapter is written by Jason G. Giorgio MBA, CFP, CLU from Pacific Advisors, Inc. He helps a significant amount of real estate professionals make the wisest choices with regards to all their financial decisions to leverage all the options available to them. We all work very hard to be successful. Having an expert team on your side to help you financially to explore all the options is an absolute must – I highly recommend Jason and his team because they deliver unprecedented results.

Learn the Rules of the Game You Are Playing

Everybody is playing a financial game they just don't realize it. If you were the coach of a football team, how would you coach your players if you didn't know how long each quarter was, or what it took to score points. The financial institutions we interact with to build our wealth are all playing by a set of rules that are really pretty simple.

Rule number one, they want our money. Rule number two, they wanted it on a recurring and regular basis. Rule number three, they want to hold onto our money for as long as possible. Rule number four, they want to give it back to us as low as slowly as possible. If we understand those rules, we can start to understand why the products in the marketplace are structured the way they are.

Think of a 401(k) retirement plan as a good example.

We contribute our money out of every paycheck to a plan that will hopefully produce good results for us 20-30 years from now, as we slowly withdraw funds at retirement. We've given up substantial elements of liquidity and access in exchange for a market based return that carries risk to us.

This is a plan that produces extremely high profits for financial institutions. Term Life insurance is another one of these vehicles where we pay a premium every month, give up control of those cash flows, and our family only receives a benefit if we die during the period of time we are covered for.

What most people don't realize is that only .3% of all term life insurance issued in this country actually pays a death benefit. So, that means that 99.7% of the time, the life insurance company gets to keep all of our contributions without having to pay a claim. Even though we might be writing relatively small insurance premium checks for this type of coverage, it actually produces the highest cost over time of any of the life insurance options available.

As a consumer, it is our responsibility to become familiar with these rules, and learn how to interact with financial institutions to win the game. As part of understanding the rules of the game, we have to also understand how the specific financial tactics we are using are either contributing to or taking away from our master strategy.

Imagine playing chess, but not being able to see the game board. You'd have no way of knowing how to position your pieces (financial products and strategies) to win the game.

Work with a Macroeconomic Financial Planner/Advisor

Almost all of us have worked with a variety of different types of professionals in the financial marketplace: CPAs attorneys, investment folks, etc. Each of these roles is important to your overall success, but often times, the scope of what they can or will do to help you is limited, and usually we're told by them that whatever product they're selling will solve whatever problem you have.

This is not an ideal way to approach your planning efforts. Enter the financial head coach of your team. This coach is responsible for coordinating not only the master plan, but also for holding an accountability role to keep all of your other "assistant coaches" on task, and accountable to the master plan.

Think of this like person like a symphony orchestra conductor. When the orchestra is warming up, you have random notes being played without coordination, and it doesn't sound great. When that same symphony is playing in coordination and cooperation, with the proper guidance, the sound is almost magical. Financial planning is really the same way. You are busy with your day to day business activities and when you get home, you also have responsibilities of family, social commitments, sporting activities, etc.

When do you have the time to also be the conductor to assess and verify that the economic decisions you are making are well coordinated, efficient, and congruent with your master plan. Most of us make our financial decisions in a very reactionary way. We are confronted with a problem or issue like sending a child to college, or planning for retirement, and so we react by making a financial decision in a vacuum, typically without consideration for the "ripple effect" that decision will have on the rest of our financial plan.

Protect Your Most Valuable Asset: You

I have asked the question of my clients many times over the years when I'm just getting to know them, "What is your most valuable asset?" People tell me my home, my retirement account, my business, etc. All the wrong answers. Your most valuable asset is you.

The time invested in your education, in gaining skills and knowledge in your trade has given you capacity to demand income from the marketplace. For some, that means you had to sacrifice for years to be where you are now. Understand, that you are the Golden Goose, and yet I find consistently, almost as a rule, that when I meet someone, they've insured some of their Golden Eggs, but have not taken the proper steps to insure and protect the lifeblood of their family's financial security, their cash flow.

Your ability to get up and go to work is your most valuable asset. None of the other assets could be built without cash flow, and none of the other assets could be maintained without cash flow. Ironically, I often find people have full coverage for their cars, homes, jewelry, etc. but have not thought about protecting their income cash flows with Disability insurance.

Most people who have coverage through work in the form of group disability or group term life insurance have never even reviewed their policy, and so their entire financial success literally hangs on the edge of a knife. The time to read about and understand the protection provided by personally or work sponsored benefits is before something happens to you. There isn't an insurance company on the planet that wants to sell you disability insurance AFTER you've gotten hurt or sick. Try having your family buy life insurance on you after your dead. Unfortunately it doesn't work that way in the marketplace.

The probability of becoming disabled during your working years is either 0% or 100% depending on who is reading this book. It will either happen to you, or it won't. Statistics say that 1 in 4 people will have a health related issue that will disable them for an average of 2 1/2 years. Some will recover and go back to work, some will stay disabled for an extended period of time, and some will die as a result of their disability.

Acquire Large Amounts of Whole Life Insurance

Despite what you might have heard from talking heads in the media, Whole Life Insurance has withstood the test of time for nearly 200 years unchanged as one of the safest and most versatile asset classes available today. I like to think of it personally as my financial Swiss Army knife. It is reliable, and as a single tool, it can accomplish almost anything I ask it to.

As one of the last remaining bastions of tax freedom, I find it is a heavily underutilized tool that has the characteristics and attributes that most people have described as characteristics "their perfect investment" would have. For example, a dollar that goes into a whole life policy, never gets taxed again if the policy is kept in force and managed properly. In most states, life insurance contracts offer substantial creditor protection.

The strong contractually guaranteed returns (usually 4% tax free by contract + an additional component of dividend return) of a whole life policy are not directly correlated to the financial markets, so as a result, the cash values within the plan which would be available to you as the policy owner won't go down unless you take the money out.

Cash Values can be withdrawn or borrowed at a moment's notice for any reason imaginable as a private transaction between you and the insurance company.

Better yet, when you "borrow" from your own policy, what actually happens is that the insurance company sends you a check out of their general account funds, while your own money sits safely in your policy still earning tax advantaged interest within the policy.

Let's look at a quick example of how this works: Let's pretend I have 100k in cash values in my whole life policy, and that money is earning me 6% tax free between the guaranteed return and a dividend that the insurance company pays me as an owner in the insurance company. Say I need 50k of that to put down on a home purchase or to finance the start of my own company.

Let's also pretend that the insurance company charges me between 4-8% depending on the contract for loans from their general account. Assuming the loan interest rate is 8%, and my policy's cash is earning 6%, my goal with the 50k I'm borrowing should be to invest it somewhere that I have the potential to earn 2% (also known as my hurdle rate) or better.

As long as I accomplish that hurdle rate, I'm able to create positive arbitrage for myself and use my money more than one time. So the math would play out like this: My 100k of Cash Value in my policy earns 6% or $6,000 for the year. The loan I took for $50,000 from the insurance company is costing me $4,000 per year in interest. The net result is I still made $2,000 overall while having the use of the $50,000 from the insurance company to purchase another asset.

On top of that, because there is no mandatory repayment schedule from a policy loan, if I want to defer any interest and principal repayment, I can do that potentially even until death when the net death benefit of the policy would repay the loan. Life insurance also allows for other types of protection built into the savings strategy.

For example, you can purchase Waiver of Premium if you qualify, which allows your systematic investment into the program to become self-completing in the event you can no longer work.

What other savings or investment company that you work with is going to continue contributing the amount you were previously contributing for you all the way to retirement? You can secure additional protections, long term care related expenses as well, access death benefits while your still alive for a variety of reasons, etc.

Unlike other forms of savings and investments, a whole life policy is a contract. It is called a unilateral contract, because once the ink is dry on the contract, you as the policyholder are the only one that can make changes to the contract as long as you pay your premiums. The insurance company can never raise rates, lower death benefits, or take away your cash values.

The most important benefit that Whole Life Insurance brings to your financial journey is the impact it has on your Retirement Distribution planning. Life Insurance provides replacement value for your income if you die prematurely, but it provides asset replacement value during the disinvestment, or retirement distribution planning phase of your life.

In other words, if I have $1 million of retirement and investment assets by the time I retire, and $1 million of whole life death benefits backing up my other assets, I can literally spend and enjoy all of my other financial assets, including principal and interest differently knowing that I have full replacement value for those assets at death.

There are only a handful of Mutual Life Insurance companies left in the marketplace that manufacture this type of insurance out of over 2,000 Insurance companies.

The probability is that if you've made insurance buying decisions, it hasn't been through one of those key companies, and as a result, you may not have Life Insurance when you need it most, and when you're most likely to pass away.

Protect your Assets from Lawsuit

I'm always surprised by the number of people I meet who have built successful entrepreneurial businesses who have not taken the steps necessary to protect those assets from confiscation due to liability or lawsuit. Like or not, we live in a very litigious society, and the better financial position you are in, the bigger the target is on your back as it relates to lawsuit risk.

The sad truth is that there are plenty of ways to further protect the valuable assets you've already put on the board, but that process is not automatic. It requires effort and good planning. Working with an asset protection attorney or specialist might save you years of effort and hard work being lost to an outside predator. Also, when structuring your entities, or legal documents such as trusts, we have the right to shop for the best jurisdiction, regardless of where we're located.

For example, Nevada has some of the strongest asset protection laws available, so many of my clients choose to form their entities or trusts in Nevada to be able to use the jurisdiction of that state to provide further protection on their money.

Save 15-20% of Your Gross Income

One of the biggest threats to our economic well-being in this country is a chronic lack of savings. As a country, we have one of the lowest average savings rates per family, usually less than 2% of gross income on average.

Whether you were a math major in college or not, it's not hard to figure out that with a level of savings like that, you will not be able to sustain a high quality of life financially when you stop working.

People I meet often have financial plans based on hope. Hope is a posture, not a strategy. There is no magic hand of the Gods that will intervene on our behalf like in the old Greek Tragedies. Countries like Japan have average savings rates of 40% or more of their gross income.

The point is, the days of the pension plan that supplemented social security are gone, and like it or not, your future success and lifestyle depends on how well you accept the personal responsibility of planning for the future. Our experience tells us that 15-20% savings rates provide at least the minimum thresholds necessary for withstanding, things like inflation, technological changes, planned obsolescence, tax changes, market volatility, etc.

These headwinds that we all face are real, and personal and discipline is the key to overcoming them. Pay yourself first, and make sure you're planning for future selves as well as your current selves.

Master the Tax Game

I would argue that most people are overpaying their taxes, and not because they love to pay taxes. There are numerous available strategies in the marketplace to help reduce or mitigate the impact of taxes.

As a firm Pacific Advisors, Inc. works with at least 15-20 key tax strategies for our clients to help them re-capture and re-purpose those inefficient dollars into more wealth to the bottom line.

How many true tax planning strategies are you taking advantage of? Most people are contributing to some sort of retirement plan, but beyond that what are you doing on a systematic basis to ensure that you have utilized the best tax strategy?

My philosophy is that we only have a right to complain about our taxes after we have thoroughly explored all of the legal options to reduce or eliminate them. Some of the less common, but most valuable tax planning ideas will never come from your CPA. CPAs are historians essentially, with a rearward looking posture in most cases. It is important that you find competent help in this domain from a qualified advanced planning tax expert.

Here is a partial list of some of the tax techniques that if you haven't explored them, you're probably missing an opportunity: Cost segregation studies for commercial real estate, qualified split interest trust planning, deferred compensation and other non-qualified benefit planning, entity layering, captive insurance companies, qualified plan optimization, TEFRA/TAMRA funded life insurance contracts, etc. Do yourself a favor, and find competent help in these domains so that you too can win the tax game.

Section V
Recommendations – Best Real Estate Resources

Corcoran Coaching and Consulting

We have been helping those in the real estate industry for over a quarter century. We assist in the growth of the precise businesses you want, and enable you to become the most successful CEO and Rainmakers of your companies. Beginning in 2011, we had the privilege of coaching 46 of the Top 250 Teams by Volume and Units as published by the Wall Street Journal & REAL Trends. In the years since, our presence on that list has increased to 81 clients that earned 102 awards in 2016. Within the first year of coaching, our clients average decreasing expenses by 23% and increasing production by 47%.

We are not an exclusive coaching company. In other words, we don't specialize in one area of growth. We work on the infrastructure through an initial intensive consultation period. We then work on moving you forward toward creating multiple pillars of revenue, which will help you achieve your goals. We will also be working with your entire team, whether it is one person or 50 people. This is 100% about what you need, and what is best for your growth.

www.CorcoranCoaching.com
Info@CorcoranCoaching.com
Phone number 800-957-8353
775 Sunset Blvd.
Suite A
O'Fallon, IL 62269

Entertainment® – VIP Perks

For over 50 years Entertainment® has been the world leader in discounts, promotions, and loyalty programs. Now you can give the value of the world's best discounts and promotions to your clients and prospects through your own custom branded rewards program. It is now also in the form of an app instead of a book. This allows you and all your clients to leverage technology to the fullest – it enables everyone to use this incredible program anywhere in the country not just their local community.

Real Estate has also been extended special pricing. To investigate this amazing program, go to the link below.   I use this powerful marketing, branding service for my own business – it is awesome!

www.VIPperks.club/Talent-Genius

VIPperks will:

- Keep your brand top of mind with your contacts
- Build your database
- Delight your best customers with real value
- Generate referrals and leads
- Drive traffic to your website
- Provide monthly communication

LinkedIn

Rhonda Sher is known as the LinkedIn Diva. She is the author of The 2 Minute Networker, the ABC's of LinkedIn - Get LinkedIn it Get Left Out and 52 Ways to Boost Business with Your Business Card. Rhonda is an expert at helping real estate professionals take their profile to profit and relationships to revenue. She is a sought after keynote speaker and trainer on the topics of Leveraging LinkedIn and How to increase your net worth with networking. She has helped hundreds of real estate professionals increase their bottom line by raising their credibility on LinkedIn.

To receive Rhonda's Resources for Realtors – Take LinkedIn to the Top – send an email to LinkedIndiva@gmail.com .

Ph #: 760-515-2822

https://www.linkedin.com/in/rhondalsher

Pacific Advisors, Inc.

Jason G. Giorgio MBA, CFP, CLU
Website: *http://www.pacificadvisors.com/jason_giorgio*
Ph #: 858-550-9338
Email address: *jason_giorgio@pacificadvisors.com*

Contact: Kim (Mo) Mahoney MBA,
Ph #:858-242-5807
Email: *mo_mahoney@pacificadvsiors.com*

Jason acts as a key advisor to Pacific Advisor's high net worth clients in the areas of advanced estate planning, business planning, and tax efficient asset management with a strong focus on protection from risk. Jason is a qualified specialist in the field of Charitable, Estate, and Business Planning, and is nationally recognized for his achievements in the financial services industry.

Jason has built his practice on helping his clients achieve their goals of accumulation, distribution, and conservation of wealth throughout their lifetimes by focusing on providing greater protection, flexibility, and control over their assets.

With the help of his planning team, Jason utilizes the most sophisticated tools and strategies available, yet does so in a way that is understandable to his clients and their other advisors. His process allows clients to re-engineer their estates and businesses to powerfully develop their ambitions for building legacy while still getting full use and enjoyment of their assets.

Jason has over 20 years of experience, continuing the Giorgio planning legacy as the third generation in his family to be involved with financial services with a bi-coastal planning practice. Jason has also been a keynote speaker on dozens of occasions for various national associations lecturing on estate planning and family business succession strategies.

Radio and Television Experts (RATE)

In the early 2000's, one brilliantly creative radio rep named Matt Wagner figured out the radio recipe for real estate agents - using an ingeniously crafted message, delivered to the right audience, by the right messenger. A dozen years, several hundred agents, and thousands of radio and television stations later, his company Radio and Television Experts is recognized as the exclusive radio and television agency of the continent's most successful real estate megastars, scores of whom have doubled and tripled their volume using RATE's media strategies.

Dave Sturgeon
VP / Director of Sales

Radio & Television Experts
74947 Hwy 111, Suite 225
Indian Wells, California

Direct: 928-920-1020

Vyral Marketing

We interview you on an HD webcam to educate your customer database with video to grow sales - we do all the work for you. We edit your videos, write your blog posts, send your emails, update your social media, and more. It only takes 30 minutes of your time per month.

Scott Sillari, VP of Business Development

Vyral Marketing
406 9th Avenue #204
San Diego, CA 92101

Tel: (858) 869-1358 | Mobile: (703) 565-7000
ssillari@getvyral.com | www.getvyral.com

Appendix A - Literature Review

Birkman-Fink, Sharon and Stephanie Capparell. The Birkman Method: Your Personality at Work, 2013.

This personality assessment method looks at your relationship with authority, communication style, response to incentives, ability to deal with change, and triggers for stress. The book explains how the factors all work together and tries to unravel the underlying motivators of satisfaction and productivity so you can gain a deeper self-awareness.

Ferguson, Matt, Lorin Hitt, and Prasanna Tambe, The Talent Equation: Big Data Lessons for Navigating the Skills Gap and Building a Competitive Workforce, 2013.

Based on a landmark big data study of more than 2,700 employers and 33 million resumes, this book is a data-driven approach to human resources. The authors were attempting to understand the relationship between market performance, education, and employee tenure and they reached some surprising conclusions. Companies can motivate employees to use their passions and gifts to create a competitive advantage. The analysis of the data in this book gives unique insights into how executives can address their staffing issues and build a dynamic and productive workforce.

Fowler, Susan. Why Motivating People Doesn't Work . . . and What Does: The New Science of Leading, Energizing, and Engaging, 2014.

Fowler uses the latest scientific research on motivation to establish her model for helping leaders guide their employees. The motivation that creates engagement and fulfillment for employees must come from the right starting point. Most leaders don't have the skills to apply the new science but her process shows how to make people less dependent on external rewards and instead create meaningful, sustainable motivation. The book is illustrated with real examples to help underscore the steps in the process she lays out.

Hartman, Robert S. The Structure of Value: Foundations of Scientific Axiology, 1967.

This book is a revolutionary work that formally explores value theory. Hartman identifies three basic kinds of value: intrinsic goods (e.g., people as ends in themselves), extrinsic goods (e.g., things and actions as means to ends), and systemic goods (conceptual values). The theory that all good things share a common structural pattern is called "formal axiology." That is not to say all things are equal—some values are richer in "good-making property-fulfillment" than others. Some sought after things, therefore, are considered better than others, which creates patterned hierarchies of value. This book establishes that how we value is just as important as what we value and so our evaluations of the hierarchies have structures and formal patterns, as well. Hartman places this in the context of historical value theory, but he goes beyond that tradition to create a new value science that has infinite applications.

Hartman, Robert S. and Arthur Ellis. The Freedom to Live, 2016.

To learn more about Hartman and his work, look for this new edition of his autobiography with additional information about his last ten years of life in the appendix. Freedom to Live: The Robert Hartman Story was written originally for presentation to management development seminars sponsored by Nationwide Insurance Company during 1962 and 1963 as a way of introducing businessmen to the man Robert S. Hartman and to his formal axiology. This book shares how the principles of value science can make the world a better and more peaceful place. Hartman's stories allow for an understanding of the past and reflection on how they can impact the world today. This is an inspiring read.

Hedge, Jason. The Essential DiSC Training Workbook: Companion to the DiSC Profile Assessment (Volume 1), 2012.

This book includes a mini DiSC assessment, but the full assessment available online will allow for more insight. To understand how you interact with others, you must first understand yourself. This knowledge will allow you to take advantage of your strengths, overcome weaknesses, and never underestimate your own abilities. Knowing yourself will also aid with effective communications with those around you. The assessment measures behaviors—what you do and how you act—which are surprisingly predictable. The workbook explains the values of the four behavioral types and the leadership aptitudes that correspond to each behavioral style. After completing this workbook, you will have a better understanding of yourself and the value others can add to your life.

Niblick, Jay. The Profitable Consultant: Starting, Growing, and Selling Your Expertise., 2013.

Niblick's book completely rethinks the traditional beliefs on how to "sell" in the consulting and coaching industry. The five-step process he lays out provides a set of rules for independent business consultants that help them to grow their practice, deliver more value, and generate more revenue. The book provides tools to help automate marketing efforts so the coach has more time to focus on generating revenue. He reviews the seven buying motives (inspired by Spranger's core dimensions) and how you can use them to highlight the value that will most appeal to each kind of person.

Jay, Niblick. What's Your Genius How the Best Think for Success. Cork: BookBaby, 2010.

This book is the result of seven years of scientific research studying the most successful business performers in the world in a wide variety of fields. It focuses on understanding personal strengths and using them to a person's advantage. Rather than trying to change how they think and make decisions—to "fix" their weaknesses—successful people put energy into trying to better apply the natural talents they already possess. Niblick helps readers identify their own "best way" of doing things, because once aligned with their natural thinking talents they will be able to perform at peak levels.

Sugerman, Jeffrey. The 8 Dimensions of Leadership: DiSC Strategies for Becoming a Better Leader, 2011.

The DiSC personality assessment helps you to understand your strengths, but to be an effective leader you need a broader perspective. This book works with those results to help you identify your primary leadership dimension—pioneering, energizing, affirming, inclusive, humble, deliberate, resolute, or commanding—and what each of those styles entails in terms of drivers, motivations, and pitfalls. The book aims to help leaders understand their own style and learn from the others to build a multidimensional approach to leadership.

Schmidt, Frank L., and John E. Hunter. "The validity and utility of selection methods in personnel psychology: Practical and theoretical implications of 85 years of research findings." Psychological Bulletin, vol. 124(2), September 1998, 262-274.

This article summarizes the practical and theoretical implications of 85 years of research in personnel selection. On the basis of meta-analytic findings, this article presents the validity of 19 selection procedures for predicting job performance and training performance and the validity of paired combinations of general mental ability (GMA) and the 18 other selection procedures. It is a landmark study of how different hiring processes can predict future job performance.

Tieger, Paul, Barbara Barron, and Kelly Tieger. Do What You Are: Discover the Perfect Career for You Through the Secrets of Personality Type, 2014.

The book includes a step-by-step assessment to discover your personality type and the types of occupations that are popular for each type. This uses work-related strengths and weaknesses and ties them into case studies for more insight.

Appendix B - Acknowledgments

I wish to personally thank the following people for their contributions to my inspiration and knowledge and other help in creating this book:

Rick Hibrant was the first manager who believed in me, thereby launching my sales career. I will always be thankful to Rick for providing me with an incredible start. Rick was an exceptional sales leader, consistently demonstrated high integrity, and was an amazing sales mentor. I am blessed our friendship has spanned over twenty-five years.

Leslie Aitken, the general manager of Learning International, put her credibility on the line and hired me as the youngest employee in company history. Leslie's deep understanding of the sales process and her amiable, likeable style made working together a pleasure. Two other exceptional people at Learning International were Terri Hebert and Jeff Shadd.

Terri's brilliant mind, business acumen, and understanding of adult learning helped me immensely. One of the nicest people you will ever meet, Terri graciously went out of her way to help accelerate my learning. Jeff Shadd was a sales legend and the number one account executive for thirteen years in a row. One of Jeff's many talents was his expertise on the art of closing a deal. His help and insight were very instrumental in my learning and sales success. There are few salespeople as highly respected or exceptional as Jeff.

Dr. Tim Daughtry is a master facilitator and expert in leadership development, organizational development, and working with senior leadership teams with strategy. He is one of the finest people I have had the privilege of working with—his influence in the early days of my career was substantial. Tim, thank you - you are first class.

One of the benefits of investing in yourself and attending personal development programs is meeting likeminded, talented people. I met Rhonda Sher over a decade ago. Little did I know she would have such an incredible impact on my personal and professional life at a time when I needed it the most. Rhonda, you are brilliant—your ability to connect the dots and introduce the best people has been a godsend. Thank you for being an exceptional chief of staff and handling all the details.

Jay Niblick is a visionary, innovative, entrepreneurial leader. Thank you for your passion and persistence in reshaping the consulting and psychometric instruments' industry. You have helped provide a more lucrative living for thousands of consultants while concurrently ensuring better outcomes and value for our clients. Beyond this, you have been a trusted ally and friend for over two decades.

The two most influential and important people in my life are my parents, Arthur and Betty Pyke. Dad, thank you for living out your faith and setting such a high standard of excellence. Your inspirational leadership, exceptional attitude in adversity, unmatched integrity, and tireless work ethic are a small sample of the rich legacy for our family to follow. My mother is one of the most tender-hearted, compassionate, thankful people I know. Mom, what a blessing it is to be your son and to be raised in such a supportive, affirming environment. Observing your personal and spiritual growth is an inspiration.

A heartfelt thanks to all the people mentioned above—your influence and contributions are woven throughout this book. And, more importantly, are carried with me day in and day out—making my life richer and more complete.

Appendix C - About the Author

John Pyke is an award-winning speaker, #1 international, bestselling author and a leading expert and advisor in the areas of hiring, sales, peak performance, employee engagement and adult learning. His work has been featured by over 200 media outlets including FOX, CBS, NBC and ABC for unprecedented sales growth and eliminating costly turnover.

Fifty percent of John's real estate clients are in the Top 250 as ranked by The Wall Street Journal Real Trends. The other fifty percent are confidently on their way there. John has helped assess, coach and hire over a quarter of a million people.

Utilizing science and statistics, John has consistently quadrupled the hiring success of his clients. John is one of the world's leading experts on hiring and sales and frequently delivers keynotes on the subjects: "Hire Fast Fire Fast – How Scientific Breakthroughs Eliminate Costly Hiring Mistakes" and "How to Sell Faster, Easier and Close More by Pushing the Buy Button in the Brain." John's personal sales performance averaged 3X his quota in his first year at five different organizations including selling more in the history of the company at two prominent sales training firms. John's MBA thesis was studying Intrinsic versus Extrinsic Motivational Factors Impacting Employee Performance.

He has been studying and researching human capital and peak performance for more than 30 years. John is married and has three children.

Since nothing is truly real until it is experienced personally, you are invited to test drive the power of these solutions firsthand. Contact John today. John can be reached at john@thetalentgenius.com or 888-846-0454.

Lightning Source UK Ltd.
Milton Keynes UK
UKOW05f1842180417

299405UK00008B/129/P

9 781539 779230